Start with Story

Start with Story

*A Practical Guide for Primary Schools:
Using Storytelling to Deepen Learning,
Improve Teaching, and Inspire Pupil Voice*

by Sita Brand and Emma Thompson
Foreword by Jean Gross CBE

© 2025 Sita Brand & Emma Thompson

The right of Sita Brand and Emma Thompson to be identified as the Author of this work has been asserted in accordance with the Copyrights, Designs and Patents Act 1988.

All rights reserved. No part of this book may be reprinted or reproduced or utilised in any form or by any electronic mechanical or other means, now known or hereafter invented, including photocopying, photographing, scanning and recording, or in any information storage or retrieval, without the permission in writing from the publisher. British Library Cataloguing in Publication Data. A catalogue record for this book is available from the British Library.

ISBN: 978-1-912121-54-0

Settle Stories Press

TABLE OF CONTENTS

Foreword   1

Introduction: The Stories That Made Us   3

Chapter 1: Why every classroom needs the magic of stories   9

Chapter 2: Your First Story Tomorrow   16

Chapter 3: The Three Questions   23

Chapter 4: The Five-Minute Planning Template   53

Chapter 5: Making It Work in Your School   63

Chapter 6: "We don't have time for stories"   78

Chapter 7: Tracking Impact   86

Chapter 8: Why This Works   95

Chapter 9: Planning Templates   104

Chapter 10: Digital Resources and Research Support   111

Appendix: Story Sources and Variations   118

References   128

About Us   130

FOREWORD

I was hooked on this book from the first moment I got into it. Why? Because it begins with a story, a personal story. A story that engaged me and made me want to hear more.

Storytelling is embedded in our evolutionary history. From the time of our earliest ancestors, stories around the campfire enabled us to better understand our world , meet its challenges and bond as a group of human beings who would look out for one another. So we survived; we lived to tell more tales.

This book is about how to use stories in the classroom, not round the campfire. But story is ever more needed in our classrooms today, where the curriculum is overloaded with facts to absorb and much of the school day is – frankly – boring. Absence rates are high, wellbeing low, behaviour problems more evident; ever more children are disengaging from learning in one way or another. We need to re-engage them, and one way to do that is to use the emotional power of narrative within our everyday teaching, within the planned curriculum.

This does not mean adding 'more' into an already crowded day or into the already exhausting Sunday-evening planning. The brilliance of this book is that it shows teachers how to use stories in ways that take up minimal time, but yield a huge return in terms of children's learning.

The book speaks to busy teachers and is wholly practical. But at the same time it is thoroughly grounded in knowledge, woven through with research nuggets for those of us who like the reassurance that evidence provides, or who are simply interested in finding out more about what works and why.

So, to finish with a story. Once upon a time... I was a primary teacher, with classes of forty lively six and seven year olds rehoused into a brand new school in a brand new town built in East London. After this I moved abroad and taught for a while, extraordinarily, in Iran in the days of the Shah; this time classes of twenty much more privileged children. Then I became a psychologist, worked in universities and local authorities and eventually got involved in leading national work on literacy, oracy and social and emotional learning. These are my passions. But if there's one thing that reading The Story-to-Curriculum Bridge made me wish, it was that I could go back in time, and back into the classroom. I would love to put the ideas into practice, and would be a much better teacher as a result.

Jean Gross CBE

"The universe is made up of stories, not atoms."

Muriel Rukeyser

Introduction

The Stories That Made Us

There was a big book of fairytales sitting on my childhood bedroom shelf in Bombay. I'd coloured in the pictures and spent hours lost in two stories particularly: Rapunzel and Bluebeard. I called her Rap-un-zel because it sounded more romantic, and I wanted straight golden hair like the girl in the picture.

My own hair was long, dark, and definitely curly. Hair that cascaded down my back and was so long I could sit on it if I leant my head back just a tiny bit. It took nearly an hour each morning to brush. It always grew out, never down. I had terrible trouble with it.

Every morning, our ayah would battle with my hair, brushing and combing and plaiting. One morning she simply wasn't there. "Bala!" I called. Nothing. She'd disappeared. not because of my impossible hair, but because a violent man had threatened her. That weekend, off to the hairdressers to have it cut short. Perhaps if I'd kept my long hair, maybe I would have had my prince.

Those stories shaped something in me. The fairytales weren't just entertainment, they were maps of possibility, warnings about the world, promises that even the most trapped person might find a way out. Marie Louise von Franz, who worked with Carl Jung, understood this: recurring motifs in traditional tales reveal shared human psychological patterns. When we tell stories, we're not just entertaining. We're tapping into ancient wisdom that still speaks to modern challenges.

The seed was planted there in Bombay, but it took decades to flower.

When everything changed

Fast forward thirty years. I'm living in the Yorkshire Dales, running Settle Stories, thinking I've found my quieter life. Then in 2016, a serious bullying incident rocked our community. The kind that has devastating consequences. Rural isolation and trauma combined in ways that damaged the mental health and wellbeing of our young people. I felt I had to act.

That's when I created The Mindful Way, an in-school project combining storytelling and mindfulness to help young people act more compassionately and find courage to stand up for themselves and others.

The response floored us. According to the Warwick Edinburgh Wellbeing scale, participant wellbeing improved from 44 points - four points below the national average - to 50.2. We'd taken Year 8 pupils above the national average for their age group in only 6 weeks.

But what struck me most wasn't the numbers. It was what the young people told us:

"A little bit more calm and controlled."
"I can handle my emotions better. I am more concentrated on my work."
"I have become more friendly to people and become more confident to talk to people and I have made several new friends."

A year later, when we met with participants, they not only remembered the stories but could retell them. They still used the exercises we'd taught them. The pilot revealed something crucial: there was an endemic problem of low self-esteem and poor mental health among our local school population. And if stories could help here, in our rural corner of Yorkshire, they could help anywhere.

Meeting Emma

That's when Emma Thompson came into the picture. Our Emma is a trained primary school teacher with years of classroom experience, someone who understood child development and knew what really worked with young children.

Emma had been watching what happened when storytellers visited her classroom. She'd seen how children who normally struggled to focus would hang on every word. How the class discussions after stories were deeper, richer. How children would reference the characters and situations for weeks afterwards.

But it was the moment she paused mid-story that convinced her. The collective groan of frustration, the urgent "Please don't stop there!" The children weren't just listening - they were invested. They didn't want to go to break because they needed to know what happened next.

Emma joined Settle Stories as our researcher and project manager, bringing her educational expertise to our growing understanding of how stories could transform learning. She became the bridge between my storytelling world and the reality of modern classrooms.

In our conversations, we discovered something powerful: when children learn concepts through stories, teachers save up to 20 minutes of explanation time because pupils grasp the ideas so much faster. The beauty of storytelling is that it makes learning click. The challenge, of course, is making it simple for teachers who aren't professional storytellers - while keeping it curriculum-friendly and sustainable in the classroom.

As Bruno Bettelheim explained in *The Uses of Enchantment,* stories help listeners find courage to face challenges in daily life. But Bettelheim was writing for parents and therapists. We needed something that worked for teachers juggling thirty children and a packed curriculum.

The bridge we built

What emerged from our collaboration was the realisation that stories aren't separate from serious learning - they enhance it. Every traditional tale contains emotional truths that children recognise instinctively. Every narrative offers multiple entry points into curriculum content.

Take *The Three Little Pigs.* In Emma's hands, it becomes a vehicle for exploring materials and their properties in science. The children aren't just learning about straw, wood, and brick - they're feeling the consequences of different choices through the pigs' experiences.

Or *The Tortoise and the Hare* for growth mindset work. Instead of abstract discussions about perseverance, children engage with characters making real choices. They debate strategy. They predict outcomes. They connect the story to their own experiences of giving up too quickly or pushing through difficulties.

The framework we developed is simple: three questions that transform any story into purposeful teaching. What's the emotional core? What's the curriculum link? What's the extension opportunity?

But simplicity took time to achieve. We tested approaches in multiple schools. We refined techniques based on what teachers actually needed, not what we thought they might want.

Why stories matter now

Children today face challenges I couldn't have imagined in that Bombay bedroom with my fairytale book. The pandemic has left many with poor mental health. Rural and urban isolation affect children differently but equally profoundly. Social media creates new forms of pressure and comparison.

Yet the fundamental human need for narrative remains unchanged. We are neurologically wired for story. Paul Zak's research demonstrates that narratives trigger the release of oxytocin, the 'trust hormone', which significantly increases empathy and social bonding. When children hear stories, they don't just listen - they simulate experiences, activate multiple brain regions, and create lasting memories through emotional engagement.

Research from Princeton neuroscientist Uri Hasson shows that during effective storytelling, the brain activities of teller and listeners literally synchronise, creating what scientists call 'neural coupling'. This shared neural experience helps explain why children remember stories long after they've forgotten facts learned through other methods.

Stories provide windows and mirrors to the world helping children see themselves reflected while encountering other perspectives. For children whose home experiences may not include rich language exposure, narrative-based approaches can help close attainment gaps.

The work continues

The success of The Mindful Way showed us we were onto something, but it also revealed how much more work needed to be done. That's why we developed The Storyful Way, an innovative programme combining storytelling, mindfulness, and creative exercises designed specifically for primary schools to encourage wellbeing and build resilience in Key Stage Two pupils.

Working alongside Emma and a team of psychologists, educators, and artists, we've created a programme that teachers can deliver confidently within their existing practice.

But our research didn't stop there. What we discovered through The Storyful Way was that the same principles that made stories so powerful for wellbeing also made them transformative for curriculum learning. Children who engaged with narrative frameworks weren't only more resilient - they were more engaged, more curious, better at making connections across subjects.

The impact of the stories experienced was seen across the curriculum.

"The children who experienced our wellbeing programmes through storytelling became better learners in everything."

"Their writing improved because they had emotional investment. Their discussions were richer because they could connect abstract concepts to character experiences. They remembered more because the learning was meaningful."

This insight led us to develop the *Start with Story,* a practical framework that takes everything we'd learned about stories' power to heal and transform lives, and applies it systematically to curriculum delivery. Not as an addition to teaching, but as a way to make teaching more effective.

"Memory is the residue of thought. Students remember what they think about, and stories provide compelling contexts for thinking about curriculum content."

D. Willingham, (2009) -
Why Don't Students Like School?

Chapter 1

Why every classroom needs the magic of stories

That little girl in Bombay, frustrated with her impossible hair, couldn't have predicted this journey. From collecting stories across the globe through my theatrical career, to settling in the Yorkshire Dales, to meeting Emma and discovering how stories could transform classroom learning.

The work we've built together - this bridge between story and curriculum - grows from understanding that narrative isn't decoration on real learning. It's how humans have always made sense of their world.

Whether we're five or fifty, facing the wolf at our door or the giant at the top of the beanstalk, stories give us frameworks for understanding our choices and their consequences. They show us that we're not alone in our struggles. They whisper the possibility that courage, kindness, and persistence might yet win the day.

Every classroom is full of storytellers waiting to discover their power. Every teacher carries narratives that could unlock learning in ways no worksheet ever could.

The question isn't whether stories belong in schools. The question is: *Which stories will you choose to tell?*

Why Story Often Gets Sidelined

Despite overwhelming evidence for its effectiveness, storytelling often ends up marginalised in primary schools. Why?

- **Time pressures:** Teachers feel every minute counts towards measurable outcomes

- **Assessment focus:** Stories feel less quantifiable than other teaching methods

- **Confidence gaps:** Not all teachers feel equipped to use storytelling strategically

- **Curriculum coverage:** Stories can seem like 'nice extras' rather than essential tools

But these concerns rest on a false premise: that stories are separate from curriculum content rather than a powerful way to deliver it.

> **Research Insight:** This isn't educational innovation—it's evidence-based restoration. From 1890-1920, storytelling was central to teacher training. Progressive Era educators like Francis Parker and John Dewey advocated oral narrative based on observations that align remarkably with modern neuroscience findings (Schatt & Ryan, 2021).

The Quiet Power of Story: Evidence from Practice

The body of research supporting narrative pedagogy is deep and diverse, providing robust justification for its systematic application across the curriculum.

Cognitive Science and Neuroscience

Based on Daniel Willingham's work, *Why Don't Students Like School?* (2009), a key finding in cognitive science is that information learned through narrative structures is retained significantly longer than information learned through abstract instruction. Experimental studies showed that students experienced 65% better retention after one week and 40% better retention after one month when using story-based learning, especially for complex or abstract concepts. As Willingham states, "Memory is the residue of thought," making stories vital as they provide compelling contexts for thinking about curriculum content.

A. Fletcher's (2023) book, *Story Thinking: The New Science of Narrative Intelligence,* reveals the profound neuroscientific impact of narrative on cognition. Drawing on research into brain activity during narrative processing, Fletcher argues that stories activate unique neural networks, including the brain's "default mode network," which is essential for creativity and insight. Unlike purely logical reasoning, narrative engagement enhances creative problem-solving, fosters empathy, and improves the ability to imagine alternative scenarios. As Fletcher states, "Stories don't just convey information - they rewire our brains for more adaptive, creative, and empathetic thinking," making strategic storytelling a vital tool for developing the cognitive flexibility required for 21st-century learning.

Language, Literacy, and Attainment

Professor Robin Alexander's (2020) work on Dialogic Pedagogy highlights the power of stories for language development. Based on an extensive observation study, Alexander found that story-based discussions produce significantly higher quality pupil talk than traditional question-and-answer sessions. During narrative discussions, pupils exhibited longer, more complex utterances and showed enhanced use of reasoning language. As Alexander notes, "Stories invite children into conversations rather than interrogations," providing the authentic context necessary for sophisticated oracy skills to flourish.

According to the Centre for Literacy in Primary Education (CLPE) findings in The Power of Reading in the Early Years, children are more deeply engaged when they encounter high-quality stories that explore strong human themes, particularly when these stories reflect aspects of their own lives, cultures, and experiences. When children see themselves represented in characters or story worlds, they form stronger emotional connections to the text, which in turn enhances their motivation to read and their overall comprehension.

A longitudinal study following children who experienced regular storytelling in primary school found lasting benefits including stronger communication skills, better emotional intelligence, and higher levels of empathy compared to control groups (Haven, 2007).

In schools serving areas of high deprivation, story-based approaches have proven particularly effective. Research by the Education Endowment Foundation's (EEF, 2021) *Arts Integration Review* shows that narrative-based teaching can help close attainment gaps, particularly for children whose home experiences may not include rich language exposure.

International Perspectives

The international significance of storytelling in education is highlighted by the *PISA (2018) Reading Literacy Framework,* which compared reading and creative thinking outcomes across 79 countries. The study found a strong correlation between an educational emphasis on storytelling and higher reading literacy scores, as well as enhanced creative thinking. As the PISA findings suggest, societies that integrate storytelling traditions into education tend to cultivate more literate, imaginative, and culturally aware citizens.

Research Summary: Key Messages

- **Memory and Retention:** Multiple studies confirm that story-based learning improves long-term retention compared to traditional instruction methods.

- **Academic Achievement:** Narrative approaches enhance rather than compete with academic outcomes, showing particular benefits for literacy, oracy, and cross-curricular understanding.

- **Inclusion and Equity:** Storytelling provides accessible entry points for all learners while developing cultural capital and supporting disadvantaged pupils.

- **Teacher Wellbeing:** Educators using storytelling approaches report increased job satisfaction and professional confidence.

- **Brain-Based Learning:** Neuroscience research confirms that emotional engagement through stories strengthens learning pathways rather than distracting from academic content.

- **International Evidence:** Countries with strong storytelling traditions in education show superior outcomes in reading, creativity, and cultural awareness.

The research consistently shows that strategic storytelling, when systematically applied through frameworks like the three-question approach, enhances educational outcomes while supporting teachers' professional satisfaction and children's personal development. This isn't about choosing between rigour and engagement - **it's about using evidence-based approaches that achieve both simultaneously.**

Stories in Action: What This Looks Like

Consider a Year 4 class exploring bravery through *Jack and the Beanstalk*. Instead of abstract discussions about courage, children engage with a character facing real choices. Should Jack climb the beanstalk? Was he brave or reckless? What would you do?

Suddenly, every pupil has something to contribute. Writing improves because children have emotional investment. Speaking and listening develops through genuine debate. PSHE objectives around decision-making and consequences emerge naturally from the story's conflicts.

This isn't about replacing curriculum content, it's about delivering it more effectively.

The Education Endowment Foundation (EEF) provides robust empirical evidence for the effectiveness of narrative-based teaching through its *Arts Integration Review* (2021). This comprehensive meta-analysis of 43 trials, involving over 20,000 pupils, found that arts-based approaches (such as drama, music, and storytelling) produce measurable gains in literacy and communication, typically equivalent to around three months' additional academic progress. These benefits were consistent across age groups, sustained over time, and particularly strong for disadvantaged pupils. The EEF concluded that arts integration strategies offer a cost-effective means of improving academic outcomes while also developing creativity and cultural capital.

What This Book Offers

This isn't a theory book arguing for storytelling's importance. It's a practical guide showing exactly how to harness a story's power for curriculum delivery.

You'll find:

- A simple three-question framework that connects any story to curriculum objectives.
- Ready-to-use examples from our Stories for Schools™ collection.

- Templates and planning tools that save time rather than create more work.
- Evidence-based approaches tested in real primary classrooms.

Because story shouldn't be something you squeeze in when there's time. It should be the foundation that makes everything else more memorable, meaningful, and engaging.

"Education should be structured as an exciting journey through the landscape of human knowledge, guided by the compass of story."

K. Egan

CHAPTER 2

Your First Story Tomorrow

Everything you need to start using strategic storytelling this week.

Right now, you might be thinking: "This all sounds lovely, but I've got thirty children, a packed curriculum, and no time to become a storyteller."

However, you don't need to become a storyteller. You already are one.

Every time you explain why the Romans built straight roads, you're telling a story. When you describe how a seed grows into a plant, you're sharing a narrative. Daily friendship issues are dealt with by helping children see why we should treat one another with kindness rather than hatred or revenge, this is human experience in action - and the learning becomes embedded.

This chapter gives you everything you need to try strategic storytelling tomorrow morning. No elaborate preparation. No performance anxiety. One story, told with clear purpose, that will show you exactly why this approach works.

The 5-Minute Starter Plan

Monday evening (5 minutes total):

   1. Choose your story (30 seconds): Pick The Three Little Pigs - you already know it

   2. Identify the emotional core (30 seconds): "Hard work and preparation pay off"

   3. Spot your curriculum link (1 minute): What are you teaching this week? Materials in science? Growth mindset in PSHE? Problem-solving in maths?

   4. Pick one extension (1 minute): Choose from the three ready-made options below

   5. Read through the story script (2 minutes): Familiarise yourself with the prompts

Tuesday morning: Tell the story using the framework below

That's it. Five minutes of planning for a lesson that will transform how your children engage with learning.

Complete Ready-to-Teach Example: The Three Little Pigs

The 2-Minute Story Script

Use your normal teaching voice. Pause where indicated. Don't worry about being theatrical.

Opening: "I'm going to tell you a story that's been shared for hundreds of years. As you listen, think about what the three pigs learn about keeping safe."

The Story: "Once upon a time, three little pigs left home to build houses of their own.

The first pig was in a hurry. He gathered straw and built his house quickly. 'There,' he said, 'now I can play all day.'

The second pig worked a bit harder. He collected sticks and built a stronger house. 'Good enough,' he decided, 'now I can relax.'

The third pig worked the longest of all. She carried heavy bricks and began building carefully. 'This will keep me safe,' she said.

Soon a hungry wolf came prowling. At the straw house, he huffed and puffed and blew it down! The first pig ran to his brother's stick house.

At the stick house, the wolf huffed and puffed harder and blew that down too! Both pigs ran to their sister's brick house.

At the brick house, the wolf huffed and puffed with all his might… but the house stood strong. The wolf gave up and went away.

The three pigs were safe, and they all learned something important that day."

Closing connection: "What did the pigs learn? How does this help us in our own lives?"

The Three Questions Applied

What's the Emotional Core? "Hard work and preparation protect us from problems"

Children understand this instinctively. They know the feeling of being rushed versus being prepared, of doing something quickly versus doing it properly.

What's the Curriculum Link? Choose the strongest connection to this week's learning:

Science - Materials Properties -"Notice how different materials behaved when the wolf tested them. Today we're going to investigate which materials are strongest."

PSHE - Growth Mindset - "The third pig didn't give up when building got difficult. She kept working because she knew it would help her. That's what we call a growth mindset."

What's the Extension Opportunity? Pick ONE of these ready-made activities:

Think: *"Which pig made the smartest choice? What would you have done?"*

- 5-minute partner discussion
- Children share one idea with the class
- Links to decision-making and consequences

Create: *"Design a house that could keep you safe from any danger"*

- 10-minute drawing activity
- Children explain their material choices
- Links to properties and design thinking

Expand on the story: *"Character Discussion"*

- Hot seating activity where one child is the wolf and others ask questions: "Why did you blow the houses down?" etc.
- Explore empathy – "Why might the wolf have acted as he did? What would you say to help him behave differently?"

Don't Have a Story? Start Here

If *The Three Little Pigs* doesn't feel right for your class, try one of these guaranteed crowd-pleasers:

Option 1: Goldilocks and the Three Bears

Emotional Core: Respecting other people's belongings and boundaries

Quick Curriculum Links:

- **PSHE:** Personal space and consent
- **Science:** Temperature (hot, cold, just right)
- **Maths:** Size comparison (big, medium, small)

Extension: Focus on Goldilocks learning that we don't take things without asking, and that everyone deserves to feel safe in their own space.

Option 2: The Tortoise and the Hare

Emotional Core: Persistence beats natural talent

Quick Curriculum Links:

- **English:** Write a letter from the hare to the tortoise asking for a rematch, using persuasive devices (rhetorical questions, emotive language, facts/opinions)
- **PE:** Pupils test different race strategies (fast start + pause vs. steady jogging) in short relays, then analyse which was most effective. (Understanding stamina, tactics, and evaluating performance)

- **Art & Design Technology:** Design a 3D trophy for the winner, with symbols (e.g., tortoise shell, hare ears) representing the qualities valued. (Product design, symbolism in art)

Extension: Emphasise the tortoise's determination and the hare's overconfidence. Perfect for children who give up quickly or compare themselves to others.

Option 3: Stone Soup

Emotional Core: Working together creates abundance

Quick Curriculum Links:

- **Science/DT:** Draw and label the cauldron as ingredients are added (Identifying food groups, ingredients, healthy eating)

- **Geography:** Explore different cultural versions of "Stone Soup" (Europe, Asia, Africa). (Learning about cultural traditions in other countries)

- **English:** Write instructions for "How to make Stone Soup" (Non-fiction writing)

2-Minute Version: Strangers help a village create a feast by encouraging everyone to contribute. Great for building classroom community and cooperation.

What to Expect

When you try this approach tomorrow, several things will probably happen:

More hands will go up during discussion than usual. The emotional connection makes children want to share their thoughts.

Children will make unexpected connections. They'll relate the story to their own experiences in ways that will continue to surprise you.

Writing or follow-up work will improve. Children produce better work when they're emotionally invested in the topic.

Classroom atmosphere will feel different. Stories create a sense of shared experience that brings classes together.

Learning will feel less rushed. The narrative framework helps children understand and remember, making your other teaching more effective.

Common First-Time Worries

"What if I forget parts of the story?" These are traditional tales - there's no "correct" version. If you miss a detail or change something, that's fine. The emotional core matters more than perfect recall.

"What if the children don't engage?" Start by sharing your own response: "This story makes me think about times when I've rushed my work and wished I'd been more careful." Children follow your lead.

"What if they ask difficult questions?" That's brilliant! Engaged questions mean the story has worked. It's fine to say "That's a really thoughtful question - what do others think?"

"What if I run out of time?" The story takes 2-3 minutes. The discussion can be as short as 30 seconds: "Turn to your partner and share one thing this story makes you think about."

Your Challenge

Try this approach once this week. Just once.

Choose *The Three Little Pigs* or pick one of the alternatives. Use the 5-minute planning format. Tell the story with your normal teaching voice. Make one curriculum connection. Try one extension activity.

Then notice what changes.

Notice how children respond during the story. Notice the quality of their questions and discussions. Notice whether they reference the story later in the week.

Because here's what teachers consistently discover: strategic storytelling doesn't add to their workload - it makes everything else work better.

Children remember curriculum content more easily when it's embedded in narrative. They engage more willingly when learning connects to universal human experiences. They try harder when they care about what they're studying.

The three-question framework simply helps you harness this power systematically, transforming storytelling from occasional treat into everyday teaching tool.

Your children are ready for their story. You have everything you need to make it matter.

What are you waiting for?

"Story is not just a delivery mechanism for information - it is a fundamental way the human brain processes and makes sense of information."

Kendal Haven

CHAPTER 3

The Three Questions

How to transform any story into purposeful teaching in under 5 minutes.

You've tried your first strategic story. Children were more engaged than usual. The discussion felt natural. Someone referenced the story later in the week.

Now you're wondering: "How do I do this with other stories? How do I make sure I'm not entertaining but actually teaching?"

This chapter gives you the simple framework that transforms any narrative into curriculum-focused learning. Three questions. Thirty seconds each. Works with any tale you know, any subject you teach, any year group you work with.

No complex planning. No curriculum wrestling. Just a systematic way to harness what stories do naturally: make learning memorable, meaningful, and personal.

> **Research Insight:** Educational research consistently shows that simple, systematic frameworks improve teacher confidence and student outcomes more than complex planning systems. Rosenshine's Principles of Instruction demonstrate that "successful teachers use systematic approaches that can be learned and applied consistently" (Rosenshine, 2012).

The Framework at a Glance

Every powerful story session needs three elements working together:

Question 1: What's the Emotional Core? *The universal human truth that makes this story stick*

Question 2: What's the Curriculum Link? *How this story supports what you're already teaching*

Question 3: What's the Extension Opportunity? *How children will actively engage with their learning*

That's it. Three questions that take 90 seconds to answer but transform passive listening into active learning.

WHAT IS THE EMOTIONAL CORE?

What it is, why children connect, and how stories develop critical thinking.

You've used the three-question framework. You've watched your class lean in during story time in ways they don't during other lessons. You've heard them reference stories days later, weaving them into playground conversations and classroom discussions.

What you've discovered is the emotional core.

Every story that survives across generations carries something that resonates beyond plot or setting. It's not the huffing and puffing that makes children remember *The Three Little Pigs* - it's the universal need to feel safe and the challenge of working out how to protect what matters. It's not magic that makes *Cinderella* compelling - it's the longing to be valued for who you really are.

When children connect with stories emotionally, something else happens. They start thinking. Fairy tale scholar Jack Zipes notes that traditional tales function as "thinking tools" - they help children analyse situations, question assumptions, and imagine alternatives. Stories don't just make children feel; they make them think.

This chapter shows you how to identify emotional cores that engage children's hearts whilst developing their minds, creating pathways to deeper thinking across your curriculum.

What Emotional Core Actually Means

Beyond Plot and Moral

Plot: What happens in the story *(Three pigs build houses, wolf arrives)*

Traditional Moral: The lesson we extract *(Work hard and you'll succeed)*

Emotional Core: The universal human experience that develops both feeling and thinking *(Needing to protect yourself and those you love, and working out the best way to do that)*

Children don't just remember how stories made them feel - they remember the thinking that emotions sparked. When they connect with a character's dilemma, they naturally start analysing: Why did this happen? What else could the character have done? How would I handle this?

The Connection: Jack Zipes observes that the best traditional tales present characters facing complex choices without obvious answers. This naturally develops children's analytical skills as they weigh options, consider consequences, and imagine alternatives.

The Recognition Test

You know you've found the emotional core when

- You feel something when you tell the story
- Children make personal connections without prompting
- Questions emerge naturally about choices and consequences
- References to the story appear when children face similar situations

If a story feels flat or your class seems disconnected, you probably haven't identified the true emotional core yet.

Quick Emotional Core Finder

The 30-Second Method

When you encounter any story, ask yourself:

"What choice or challenge is at the heart of this tale?"

Then complete: **"This story is really about… [situation that requires thinking]"**

Examples:

Jack and the Beanstalk

- *Plot*: Boy climbs beanstalk, encounters giant
- *Emotional Core:* "This story is really about… taking risks when your family needs help, and working out what's worth the danger"

The Ugly Duckling

- *Plot:* Young bird looks different, gets rejected, transforms
- *Emotional Core:* "This story is really about… staying true to yourself

when others make you feel like you don't belong, and learning to recognise your own worth"

The Sun and the Wind

- *Plot:* Sun and Wind argue about who is stronger, compete to make traveller remove coat

- *Emotional Core:* "This story is really about... discovering that gentle, patient approaches often succeed where force and aggression fail, and learning when to use warmth instead of power"

When You're Stuck

Try these thinking-focused prompts:

"What decision does the main character have to make?" Stories that engage children intellectually involve choice points.

"What problem needs solving?" The best emotional cores involve challenges that require creative thinking.

"What question does this story raise?" Strong emotional cores make children wonder "What would I do?"

"How does this character work things out?" The thinking process is often as important as the outcome.

> **Research Insight:** Jerome Bruner's distinction between "paradigmatic" (logical) and "narrative" (story-based) thinking shows that children naturally process emotional and social understanding through stories before they can handle abstract moral reasoning. The emotional core provides the bridge between concrete experience and abstract values.

Common Emotional Cores That Develop Critical Thinking

Problem-Solving Under Pressure

Stories where characters must think their way through difficult situations:

- **Anansi and the Wisdom Pot:** Discovering that hoarding knowledge creates problems, while sharing it brings solutions - and learning to adapt when plans go wrong

- **Molly Whuppie:** Outwitting a giant through courage, strategy, and persistent problem-solving across multiple challenges

- **Hansel and Gretel:** Using available resources creatively to escape danger

Critical Thinking Development: Children learn to evaluate options, predict consequences, and adapt strategies when initial plans don't work.

Understanding Different Perspectives

Tales that present multiple viewpoints on the same situation:

- **The Three Billy Goats Gruff:** Considering why someone might guard a bridge and whether there are alternatives to conflict

- **The Gingerbread Man:** Considering why different characters chase him and what motivates their actions

- **The Boy Who Cried Wolf:** Analysing how trust works and what happens when communication breaks down

Critical Thinking Development: Children practise perspective-taking, empathy, and understanding cause-and-effect relationships.

Questioning Assumptions

Stories that challenge obvious answers or simple categorisations:

- **The Blind Men and the Elephant:** Understanding that everyone may have part of the truth, and our limited perspective doesn't show the whole picture

- **Beauty and the Beast:** Looking beyond surface appearances to understand character

- **The Emperor's New Clothes:** Challenging groupthink and the courage to speak truth when everyone else stays silent

Critical Thinking Development: Children learn to look deeper than first impressions and question easy answers.

Exploring Fairness and Justice

Traditional tales survived because they helped people think through complex social and moral questions. The same stories that engaged our ancestors' critical thinking can develop these skills in modern children. Tales that present moral dilemmas without simple solutions:

- **Robin Hood:** Analysing when rules should be followed and when they should be challenged

- **Cinderella:** Understanding how systems can be unfair and imagining how they might change

- **The Little Red Hen (European/American):** Understanding fairness in work and reward - who deserves the benefits when not everyone contributes equally

Critical Thinking Development: Children practise moral reasoning, consideration of multiple stakeholders, and systemic thinking.

Traditional tales survived because they helped people think through complex social and moral questions. The same stories that engaged our ancestors' critical thinking can develop these skills in modern children.

Helping Children Connect and Think

Create Safe Thinking Space

Before the story: "This tale has made people think for hundreds of years. As you listen, notice what questions it raises for you."

During the story: Pause at decision points: "What would you do here? What are the character's options?"

After the story: "What did this story make you wonder about?" rather than "What's the moral?"

Develop Critical Thinking Through Questions

Analysis Questions:

- "Why do you think the character made that choice?"
- "What else could they have done?"
- "What would happen if...?"

Synthesis Questions:

- "How is this similar to other stories we know?"
- "Where do we see this kind of situation in real life?"
- "What pattern do you notice in how this character solves problems?"

Evaluation Questions:

- "Do you think that was the best solution? Why?"
- "What would you have done differently?"
- "How could we test whether this approach would work?"

Creation Questions:

- "What would happen next in this story?"
- "How would this story be different if…?"
- "What would a different character do in this situation?"

Age-Appropriate Critical Thinking Development

EYFS/Year 1: Focus on choice recognition and simple analysis

- "The character had to choose between… Which do you think was better?"
- "What happened because the character did that?"
- "How do you think they worked out what to do?"

Years 2-3: Explore alternatives and consequences

- "What are three different things the character could have done?"
- "Why do you think they chose this option instead of the others?"
- "What questions would you ask this character about their decision?"

Years 4-6: Examine complex reasoning and systemic thinking

- "What assumptions is this character making? Are they correct?"
- "How do different characters' actions affect each other?"
- "What would need to change for this story to end differently?"
- "How does this story help us think about similar situations today?"

Case Study: Critical Thinking Through Emotional Core

The Challenge

Amira teaches Year 4 in an inner-city school where pupils often respond impulsively. In discussions, they jump to conclusions instead of weighing alternatives. In their storytelling, characters' actions can feel random, with little sense of cause and effect. In science investigations, children sometimes rush to test an idea without considering safer or more effective approaches.

The Approach

Amira chose *Little Red Riding Hood,* but she focused on the inner dilemmas and choices that drive the story, rather than the moral lesson alone.

Emotional Core:
"When you're faced with curiosity or temptation, how do you decide whether to follow your feelings, or to step back and think first?"

Critical Thinking Focus:
Evaluating risks and benefits, questioning appearances, and testing assumptions through the characters' decisions.

The Session

Before the story:
Amira asked: "Sometimes we want to do something that feels exciting or safe, but we don't always think ahead. As you listen, ask: what choices do these characters really have, and how do they weigh up their decisions?"

During the story (pausing at decision points):

- **When Little Red Riding Hood leaves the path:**
  "Why might she be tempted to stray? What did she assume about the safety of the forest? What alternatives were open to her?"

- **When she meets the wolf:**
  "Should she trust a stranger who seems friendly? What questions could she ask to check if her assumptions are right?"

- **When the wolf suggests visiting the flowers/grandmother:**
  "What hidden consequences might come from following his idea? How could she test whether his suggestion is safe?"

- **When the grandmother faces the wolf:**
  "What strategies could she use to protect herself? Are there creative or less obvious options?"

Critical thinking moment:
As Little Red Riding Hood notices something strange about "Grandmother":
"What clues should she look for to test her assumptions? How might she gather more evidence before it's too late?"

"If you were in her place, how could you check whether your plan to escape might succeed?"

After the story:
Amira asked: "Which characters thought carefully before acting? Who jumped too quickly into decisions? What thinking tools—like questioning, testing, or predicting—might have helped them make better choices?"

Extensions That Developed Thinking

- **Analysis Extension:** Children mapped out each character's choices, showing *what they knew, what they assumed, and what they ignored.*

- **Evaluation Extension:** Children created a "Decision-Making Checklist" with questions like: *What are my options? What's the evidence for each? What could go wrong?*

- **Synthesis Extension:** Children applied this checklist in other subjects:

- **In science:** predicting which materials might change under heat and why.

- **In maths:** deciding which operation makes sense before calculating.

- **In PSHE:** exploring friendship dilemmas where quick choices could backfire.

The Results

Immediate: Children slowed down their thinking, offering multiple options for each decision point rather than jumping to the obvious.

Writing improvement: Characters became more layered, with dilemmas, second thoughts, and consequences.

Science connections: During investigations, children began to ask: *"What's the evidence? Could there be another explanation?"*

Cross-curricular transfer: In history, they questioned whether a source might be misleading; in maths, they checked if an answer was reasonable before finalising it.

Long-term impact: Children adopted the shared vocabulary of "hidden options" and "checking consequences," helping them reflect more deeply across tasks.

The Lesson

By anchoring critical thinking in the *emotional core of pressure and consequences,* Amira helped children practise decision-making skills that reached far beyond the fairy tale. The story became a rehearsal space for analysing choices, predicting outcomes, and evaluating evidence—habits of mind that transferred to every subject.

Building Your Critical Thinking Story Collection

Look for Stories That Require Analysis

Problem-solving stories: Characters face challenges that require creative thinking

> • **Rumpelstiltskin:** How do you solve an impossible problem?

> • **The Enormous Turnip:** When do you need help and how do you organise cooperation?

Perspective stories: Multiple viewpoints on the same events

> • **The True Story of the Three Little Pigs:** How do different narrators shape our understanding?

> • **Little Red Riding Hood:** What happens when we consider the wolf's motivations?

Choice stories: Characters must make difficult decisions

> • **The Fisherman and His Wife:** When is enough enough?

> • **Jack and the Beanstalk:** How do you weigh risk against potential benefit?

Questions That Develop Critical Thinking

For any story, ask:

> • What problem is the character trying to solve?

- What information do they have to work with?
- What assumptions are they making?
- What alternatives did they consider?
- How do they know if their solution worked?
- What would happen if circumstances were different?

Connect to Real-World Thinking

Help children see stories as practice for real-world analysis:

- Scientific method (hypothesis, prediction, testing)
- Historical thinking (cause and effect, multiple perspectives)
- Mathematical reasoning (pattern recognition, logical steps)
- Design thinking (problem definition, ideation, iteration)

When Stories Don't Develop Thinking

Common Problems and Solutions

Problem: *"Children just want to know what happens next"*

Solution: Pause frequently to ask prediction questions with reasoning: "What do you think will happen? What makes you think that?"

Problem: *"Children give simple, obvious answers"*

Solution: Ask follow-up questions: "What other possibilities are there? What if the character tried a different approach?"

Problem: *"Discussions don't go deeper than surface reactions"*

Solution: Model analytical thinking: "I'm wondering why the character made that choice. Let me think about what they knew and what they were trying to achieve…"

Your Critical Thinking Challenge

Choose one story you know well and apply this enhanced emotional core approach:

1. Identify the thinking challenge at the story's heart

2. Plan pause points where characters face decisions or solve problems
3. Prepare analytical questions that require reasoning beyond plot recall
4. Try it with your class and notice:

- What kinds of thinking children demonstrate
- How they approach problems in other subjects afterward
- Whether they use story references when facing real challenges
- How their question-asking develops

Because when children connect emotionally with stories that require thinking, they develop both heart and mind. They learn that feelings and analysis work together, that caring about outcomes motivates better thinking, and that stories provide safe spaces to practise the kind of reasoning they'll need throughout their lives.

The emotional core isn't separate from critical thinking - it's the engine that drives it. When children care about characters and their dilemmas, they naturally want to think more deeply, question more thoroughly, and imagine more creatively.

That's why the emotional core comes first in your framework. It creates the conditions where critical thinking flourishes naturally, making every story a tool for developing the analytical minds your children need for the complex world they're inheriting.

Fairy tale scholar Jack Zipes notes that traditional tales have always been "thinking tools" that help people analyse complex situations. When we use stories this way in education, we're continuing an ancient tradition whilst developing 21st-century critical thinking skills.

WHAT IS THE CURRICULUM LINK?

How to spot natural connections, avoid forced fits, and make stories work for every subject.

You've identified the emotional core of your story. Children are engaged, connected, ready to learn. Now comes the crucial question: how does this story support what you actually need to teach?

This is where many teachers stumble. They either force awkward connections that confuse children about what they're supposed to be learning, or they give up on curriculum links altogether and treat stories as separate from "real" teaching.

Both approaches miss the point. The best curriculum connections feel so natural that children don't realise they're learning through stories - they're just learning, deeply and memorably, because the story provides the perfect context.

This chapter shows you how to spot these authentic connections quickly and consistently.

The Natural Connection Test

A good curriculum link should feel **inevitable**, not clever.

When you tell *The Three Little Pigs* during your materials science unit, children should think: "Of course we're testing which materials are strongest - the story made me wonder about that."

When you use *Stone Soup* for your history work on communities, the connection should be obvious: "Of course we're thinking about how people worked together in the past - that's exactly what this story shows."

Signs of a Natural Connection

✓ **Good Links:**

- The story **illuminates** the curriculum content
- The curriculum content **deepens** understanding of the story
- Children make the connection **without prompting**

- The link feels **obvious** once you point it out

✗ **Forced Links:**
- You have to **explain** why they connect
- The story could link to **anything** with enough creativity
- Children look **confused** about what they're supposed to learn
- You feel like you're **stretching** to make it work

The One-Connection Rule

Choose ONE strong link, not three weak ones.

Every story could theoretically connect to multiple subjects. *Goldilocks* touches on size comparison (maths), temperature (science), respect for property (PSHE), and descriptive writing (English).

But trying to cover everything means covering nothing well.

Instead: Pick the most natural, meaningful connection for this week's learning. Explore it properly. Let other connections emerge organically if children spot them, but don't force them.

Subject-by-Subject Quick Reference

English Connections

- **Character Analysis:** Identify the hero, villain, and supporting characters. Describe traits, motives, and actions. Compare two characters (good vs. evil) using adjectives and evidence from the text.

- **Setting Exploration:** Discuss where the story takes place. Draw or write a detailed description of the setting using adjectives and expanded noun phrases. Change the setting (e.g. forest changed to space) and predict how the story would change.

- **Problem and Resolution Mapping:** Identify the main problem in the story. Make a "problem–solution chart" showing the conflict and how it is resolved. Explore alternative endings with different solutions.

- **Magical Elements:** Identify magical objects, animals, or powers in the tale. Discuss how magic changes the story or characters' actions. Invent a new magical element and write a scene including it.

- **Moral / Lesson:** Discuss what the story teaches. Write a sentence summarizing the moral in your own words. Compare morals across two different tales and discuss similarities.

Science Connections

Look for stories with embedded scientific concepts:

Materials and Properties

- *The Gingerbread Man:* How materials change when heated (baking, melting), irreversible changes
- *The Three Billy Goats Gruff:* What makes bridges stable?

Life Cycles and Growth

- *Jack and the Beanstalk:* What do plants need to grow?
- *The Ugly Duckling:* How do animals change as they develop?

Forces and Movement

- *The Sun and the Wind:* Different types of energy and their effects
- *The Tortoise and the Hare:* Speed, distance, and movement

Habitats and Adaptation

- *Little Red Riding Hood:* Forest ecosystems and animal behaviour
- *The Three Bears:* How animals adapt to their environments

History Connections

Focus on universal human experiences across time:

Community Life

- *Stone Soup:* How did communities support each other in the past?
- *Robin Hood:* What was life like for different social classes?

Values and Beliefs

- *King Arthur tales:* What did people value in medieval times?
- *Biblical stories:* How did beliefs shape daily life?

Decision-Making and Consequences

- *Any traditional tale:* How do people make choices when facing difficulty?

- *Perfect for:* Understanding historical decisions, cause and effect

Change and Continuity

- *Folktales from different eras:* What stays the same about human nature across time?

PSHE Connections

Stories are natural vehicles for exploring relationships and values:

Emotional Development

- *The Ugly Duckling:* Identity and self-acceptance
- *The Boy Who Cried Wolf:* Trust and honesty in relationships

Moral Reasoning

- *Jack and the Beanstalk:* When is taking risks justified?
- *Cinderella:* How should we treat people fairly?

Relationships and Community

- *Stone Soup:* Cooperation and contribution
- *The Lion and the Mouse:* How we can all help each other

British Values

- *Robin Hood:* Democracy and justice
- *Any fairness tale:* Rule of law and equality

Making Connections Feel Natural

Before the Story

Set up the learning context first: "We've been learning about materials and which ones are strong. I'm going to tell you a story that will help us think about this..."

Rather than: "I'm going to tell you a story and then we'll do some science."

During the Story

Pause at key moments to highlight connections: "Notice how the wolf's huffing and puffing affects different materials. What does this tell us about their properties?"

Ask connecting questions: "Why do you think the brick house stayed strong when the others didn't?"

After the Story

Make the curriculum link explicit: "So what did this story teach us about materials? How can we use this understanding in our investigation?"

Subject-Specific Examples in Practice

Science Example: *The Three Billy Goats Gruff*

Emotional Core: Standing up to bullies and protecting those smaller than yourself

Natural Science Link: Forces and structures - what makes bridges strong?

Implementation:

- **Before:** "We're investigating forces this week. This story will help us think about what happens when forces act on structures."

- **During:** Pause when each goat crosses: "What forces are acting on the bridge? Why doesn't it break?"

- **After:** "Let's test what makes bridges strong using our own materials."

- **Extension:** Children build and test bridges, applying story insights about weight, materials, and structural stability.

History Example: *Stone Soup*

Emotional Core: Community cooperation creates abundance

Natural History Link: How did communities work together in the past?

Implementation:

- **Before:** "We're learning about how people lived in villages long ago. This story shows us how communities survived difficult times."

- **During:** Pause when villagers contribute: "Why were people suspicious of strangers? How did sharing help everyone?"

- **After:** "How is this similar to communities we've studied? What other examples of cooperation do we know from history?"

- **Extension:** Children research examples of community cooperation in their local area's history.

PSHE Example: *The Pied Piper of Hamelin*

Emotional Core: When communities break promises and fail to value others' contributions, everyone suffers the consequences

Natural PSHE Link: Keeping promises, community responsibility, justice and fairness, consequences of decisions, respecting others' work

Implementation:

- **Before:** "We're exploring what happens when people in power don't keep their word, and why communities need to treat everyone fairly."

- **During:** Pause at critical moments: "The Mayor promised payment - why might he break that promise? What power does the Piper have now? Who suffers most from the adults' choices?"

- **After:** "Was the Piper's revenge justified? What responsibility did the townspeople have? How could this have been prevented? Where do we see similar situations today?"

- **Extension:** Children debate the moral complexity - was anyone completely right or wrong? They write persuasive letters from different perspectives (the Mayor justifying his decision, parents pleading for their children's return, the Piper explaining his actions), or create a "community contract" outlining how groups should treat those who help them.

No clear curriculum connection this week? Choose from these always-relevant areas:

- **Speaking and Listening:** Every story develops oracy skills
- **PSHE:** Every story explores human experience
- **English:** Every story teaches narrative structure
- **Cultural Capital:** Traditional tales build cultural knowledge

Subject-Specific Support

Stories for Schools™ provides comprehensive curriculum mapping for each Key Stage, showing exactly which stories support which statutory objectives across:

- **National Curriculum subjects:** Clear links to specific learning objectives

- **Assessment criteria:** How story-based learning supports progress measures

- **Cross-curricular opportunities:** Natural connections between subjects

- **Progression planning:** How the same stories can support different year groups

This means you never have to guess whether a story will support your curriculum requirements - the connections are mapped, tested, and ready to use.

Your Planning Challenge

Look at next week's curriculum planning. Choose one subject area where children need additional support or engagement.

1. Identify the specific learning objective you need to address
2. Choose a story that naturally connects to this learning (use the subject reference above)
3. Apply the natural connection test: Does the link feel inevitable rather than clever?
4. Plan using a template

Try it once this week. Notice how much easier it is to engage children when the story and curriculum genuinely support each other.

Because when connections are natural, something magical happens: children stop seeing stories and subjects as separate things. Instead, they experience learning as connected, meaningful, and memorable.

That's the power of authentic curriculum links - they make learning more engaging and more effective.

WHAT IS THE EXTENSION OPPORTUNITY?

How to transform passive listening into active learning through thinking, creating, and acting.

Your story has landed. Children are emotionally connected through the core you identified. They understand the curriculum link you've made explicit. Now comes the moment that determines whether this becomes memorable learning or just another nice story.

What happens next?

Too often, nothing. The story ends, children enjoy it, and everyone moves on to maths worksheets or spelling practice. The emotional engagement and curriculum connection get wasted because there's no bridge from listening to learning.

Extension opportunities are that bridge. They transform passive listeners into active learners by giving children ways to think, create, or act based on what the story has taught them.

This chapter shows you how to design extensions that deepen understanding, support assessment, and make story-based learning stick long after the telling ends.

The Three Types of Extension

✓ **Think: Discussion and Philosophy**

What it is: Children explore ideas, debate perspectives, make connections

When to use: When your curriculum link involves reasoning, problem-solving, or understanding different viewpoints

Examples:

- **Philosophy circles:** "What makes someone brave?"

- **Perspective-taking:** "How would the giant feel about Jack's actions?"

- **Modern connections:** "Where do we see this happening today?"

- **Moral reasoning**: "Was the character right to...?"

✓ **Create: Art, Writing, and Drama**

What it is: Children express understanding through making something

When to use: When your curriculum link involves communication, design, or demonstrating knowledge

Examples:

- Drawing from different perspectives
- Writing in role as characters
- Designing solutions to story problems
- Creating artwork inspired by themes
- Performing alternative endings

✓ **Act: Investigation and Real-World Application**

What it is: Children test ideas, research further, or apply learning practically

When to use: When your curriculum link involves scientific concepts, historical inquiry, or applying the learning to real-life situations

Examples:

- Growing plants after *Jack and the Beanstalk*
- Planning a community food activity after *Stone Soup*
- Investigating forces after *The Sun and the Wind*

Choosing the Right Extension Type

Match Extension to Curriculum Link

Science Link Act: Test, investigate, explore

- *The Enormous Turnip* (forces) Investigate how many people it takes to move objects of different weights, measure pulling forces
- *Jack and the Beanstalk* (plants) Grow beans in different conditions

PSHE Link Think: Discuss, reflect, apply to real situations

- *The Boy Who Cried Wolf* (honesty and trust) Discuss how trust is built and broken: "How long does it take to build trust? How quickly can it be lost? What can we do to rebuild trust when it's damaged?"

• *The Lion and the Mouse* (kindness and helping others) Philosophy circle: "Can small actions make big differences? When should we help someone even if there's nothing in it for us? What does it mean to be kind?"

English Link Create: Write, draw, perform

• *Any traditional tale* Write alternative endings or character diaries

• *Stories with rich settings* Create detailed descriptions or artwork

History Link Act: Research, investigate, compare

• *The Great Fire of London stories* (historical events) Compare eyewitness accounts from Samuel Pepys' diary with the story versions, examining what's fact vs. narrative

• *Robin Hood* (medieval life) Investigate what life was really like

The 10-Minute Rule

Most effective extensions take **5-10 minutes** and feel like natural responses to the story.

Too brief (under 3 minutes): Doesn't allow deep thinking or quality creation

Too long (over 15 minutes): Dominates the session and feels separate from the story

Just right (5-10 minutes): Deepens understanding without overwhelming the narrative experience

Thinking Extensions: Going Deeper

Philosophy Circles

Perfect for: Stories with moral dilemmas or big questions about life

How it works:

1. Sit in a circle (or small groups)
2. Pose one open question based on the story
3. Children share thoughts without judgment
4. Build on each other's ideas
5. No need to reach conclusions - the thinking matters most

Example: *The Tortoise and the Hare*

- Question: "Is it better to be naturally talented or to work hard?"
- Follow-ups: "Can you be both? Which matters more for earning? What about for friendship?"

Example: *Jack and the Beanstalk*

- Question: "When is it okay to take risks?"
- Follow-ups: "What if your family needed help? What if someone might get hurt? How do we decide?"

Perspective-Taking

Perfect for: Stories with multiple characters or potential viewpoints

How it works:

1. Choose a character other than the main one
2. Children discuss or write about the story from their perspective
3. Compare different viewpoints
4. Explore how perspective changes understanding

Example: *The Three Little Pigs*

- Wolf's perspective: "I was just hungry and looking for dinner. Why were these pigs so mean to me?"
- Second pig's perspective: "I thought my stick house was good enough. I learned I need to plan more carefully."

Example: *Goldilocks and the Three Bears*

- Baby Bear's perspective: "Someone came into my home and broke my special chair. How would you feel?"
- Goldilocks' parents' perspective: "Our daughter went missing in the woods. We were so worried."

Modern Connections

Perfect for: Traditional tales with timeless themes

How it works:

1. Identify the core situation from the story
2. Help children recognise similar situations today

3. Discuss how story wisdom applies to modern life
4. Make it relevant to their experiences

Example: *The Boy Who Cried Wolf*

- Modern connection: "Where do we see people not being believed today? What about on social media? How can we build trust?"

Example: *Stone Soup*

- Modern connection: "How do communities work together now? What about food banks, community gardens, or fundraising?"

Creative Extensions: Showing Understanding

Artistic Response

Perfect for: Stories with vivid imagery or strong emotions

Quick Options:

- **Draw the feeling:** "Show me what courage/loneliness/joy looks like"

- **Character portraits:** "Draw the character at the beginning vs. the end"

- **Setting creation:** "Design the perfect home for this character"

- **Story maps:** "Show the character's journey through the tale"

Example: *The Ugly Duckling* - Children create "belonging" artwork - places, people, or situations where they feel they belong. Connects art skills with emotional understanding.

Writing in Role

Perfect for: Stories where children connect strongly with characters

Quick Options:

- **Diary entries:** What would the character write about this experience?

- **Letters:** Character writes to someone about what happened

- **Alternative endings:** What if the character made a different choice?

- **Prequel/sequel:** What happened before or after the story?

Example: ***Jack and the Beanstalk*** - Children write Jack's letter to his mother explaining why he traded the cow for beans. Develops persuasive writing while exploring character motivation.

Drama and Performance

Perfect for: Action-packed stories or tales with strong dialogue

Quick Options:

- **Freeze frames:** Show key moments from the story
- **Conscience alley:** Character walks between two lines hearing advice
- **Hot seating:** Interview characters about their choices
- **Alternative scenes:** What if characters met in different circumstances?

Example: ***The Sun and the Wind*** - Children create short scenes showing "Sun approaches" vs "Wind approaches" in school situations - asking to join a game, resolving conflicts, persuading someone to help.

Action Extensions: Real-World Application

Example: Local Legends or Folktales Project: "Preserving Our Community Stories"

- **Identify:** Elderly community members, local historians, archives with stories to share

- **Plan:** Interview training, recording equipment, story collection framework

- **Act:** Conduct interviews, transcribe stories, create digital archive or published booklet

- **Reflect:** Why is it important to preserve these stories? What did we learn about our community?

- **Sustain:** Annual story collection project, partnership with local library/museum, story-sharing events

Example: ***The Enormous Turnip Project:*** "It Takes Everyone - School Garden Initiative"

- **Identify:** Unused school space that could become a garden or wildlife area

- **Plan:** Different classes take responsibility for different aspects (digging, planting, watering, harvesting)

- **Act:** Create community growing space, donate produce to local food bank or school lunches

- **Reflect:** What could we achieve together that no one could do alone?

- **Sustain:** Garden maintenance rota, seasonal planting plans, garden club

Assessment Through Extensions

Extensions provide natural assessment opportunities without formal testing.

What to Look For

Understanding: Can children apply story insights to new situations?

Connection-Making: Do they link story themes to their own experiences or other learning?

Creativity: Are they finding original ways to express their thinking?

Depth: Do their responses show surface-level or deeper understanding?

Evidence Collection

Think Extensions:

- Record key quotes from discussions
- Note children who make unexpected connections
- Observe who builds on others' ideas

Create Extensions:

- Keep examples of artwork or writing that show deep understanding
- Photo drama work or performances
- Note children's explanations of their creative choices

Act Extensions:

- Document investigation processes and conclusions
- Record children's ability to apply story learning to real situations
- Note collaboration and problem-solving skills

Making Assessment Natural

- **Avoid:** "I'm going to assess your understanding of the story"
- **Avoid:** Formal rubrics and criteria during the extension
- **Avoid:** Making every extension into an assessment opportunity

- **Instead:** "Show me what this story made you think about"
- **Instead:** Notice authentic responses and record observations afterward
- **Instead:** Sometimes let children explore without evaluation

Common Extension Challenges

"Children rush through to get to the 'fun part'"

Solution: Make the story itself engaging enough that the extension feels like a natural continuation, not a reward for listening.

"Some children don't engage with extensions"

Solution: Offer choice between Think, Create, and Act. Ensure extensions match your curriculum link so they feel purposeful rather than optional.

"Extensions feel disconnected from the story"

Solution: Make explicit connections: "This investigation helps us understand what the pigs learned about materials" rather than "Now we're going to do some science."

Building Your Extension Library

Start collecting effective extensions by:

Story theme: What extensions work well for courage stories? Fairness stories? Growth stories?

Curriculum area: What Think/Create/Act options support science learning? History learning? PSHE learning?

Practical needs: What extensions require no resources? What can be done in small spaces? What works with large classes?

Time available: 5-minute options for busy days, 15-minute options for deeper exploration

Your Extension Challenge

Choose one story you've told recently (or plan to tell this week):

1. **Identify the curriculum link** you made or want to make
2. **Choose the most suitable extension type:** Think for reasoning, Create for expression, Act for investigation
3. **Design a 5-10 minute extension** that feels like a natural response to the story
4. **Try it with your class** and notice:

- How engaged children are

- What their responses reveal about their understanding

- Whether the extension deepens or distracts from learning

Because well-designed extensions are what transform story sessions from entertainment into education. They're the bridge between emotional engagement and lasting learning.

When children think deeply about story themes, create responses that show their understanding, or act on story insights in the real world, they're not just enjoying tales - they're developing as learners and human beings.

That's the power of purposeful extension opportunities. They turn every story into a doorway to deeper understanding.

"People forget facts but they remember stories."

Joseph Campbell

CHAPTER 4

The Five-Minute Planning Template

The tool that makes strategic storytelling as quick as choosing a worksheet.

You understand the three questions. You've tried the framework. It works.

But you're still spending too much time thinking through each story session. You need something faster, more systematic, that fits into your existing planning routine.

This chapter gives you the template that experienced teachers use to plan story sessions in under five minutes. Plus two complete examples you can use immediately, showing exactly how to apply the template to different stories and year groups.

By the end of this chapter, you'll have a planning tool that makes strategic storytelling as quick and reliable as any other teaching method you use.

THE TEMPLATE

Story Planning Sheet

Story Title: _____ Date: _____

Year Group: _____ Duration: _____ Subject Focus: _____

Question 1: What's the Emotional Core?

Complete: "This story teaches us that..."

Question 2: What's the Curriculum Link?

This week's learning objective that connects naturally:

Subject: _____

Specific Objective: _____

Connection: _____

Question 3: What's the Extension Opportunity?

Choose ONE:

Think: Discussion/Philosophy *(What will children discuss?)*

Create: Art/Writing/Drama *(What will children make?)*

Act: Investigation/Real-world *(What will children explore?)*

Specific Activity: _____

Story Notes:

Key moments to pause, questions to ask, connections to highlight

Success Indicators:

How will you know this worked?

For access to the editable templates Join Stories for Schools™

Complete Example 1: *Jack and the Beanstalk*

Story Planning Sheet

Story Title: Jack and the Beanstalk **Date:** Monday Week 3

Year Group: Year 2 Duration: 15 minutes **Subject Focus:** Science

Question 1: What's the Emotional Core?

Complete: "This story teaches us that…"

This story teaches us that sometimes we need courage to help the people we love, even when we're scared.

Question 2: What's the Curriculum Link?

This week's learning objective that connects naturally:

Subject: Science

Specific Objective: Observe and describe how seeds and bulbs grow into mature plants

Connection: Jack's magic beans grow into an enormous plant overnight. We can explore what plants need to grow and observe our own bean investigation.

Question 3: What's the Extension Opportunity?

Choose ONE:

Think: Discussion/Philosophy

Create: Art/Writing/Drama

Act: Investigation/Real-world

Specific Activity: Plant our own beans in different conditions (light/dark, water/no water) and measure growth over two weeks. Predict which will grow the tallest.

Story Notes:

Key moments to pause, questions to ask, connections to highlight

- Pause when Jack plants the beans: "What do you think plants need to grow?"
- When beanstalk appears: "How did it grow so fast? What helped it?"

- Emphasise Jack's climb: "That took courage. When do we need to be brave?"

- Connect to our investigation: "Let's see if we can grow beanstalks too"

Success Indicators:
How will you know this worked?

Children make predictions about plant growth, understand that plants need certain conditions, and show excitement about growing their own beans.

For ready-made templates join Stories for Schools™.

Complete Example 2: *The Sun and the Wind*
Story Planning Sheet
Story Title: The Sun and the Wind **Date:** Thursday Week 1

Year Group: Year 4 **Duration:** 20 minutes **Subject Focus:** PSHE

Question 1: What's the Emotional Core?
Complete: "This story teaches us that..."

This story teaches us that gentle approaches often work better than force when we want to influence others.

Question 2: What's the Curriculum Link?
This week's learning objective that connects naturally:

Subject: PSHE

Specific Objective: Learn about different types of relationships and how to maintain positive relationships

Connection: The story shows two different approaches to getting what you want from others. Links to our work on friendship skills and resolving conflicts peacefully.

Question 3: What's the Extension Opportunity?

Choose ONE:

Think: Discussion/Philosophy

Create: Art/Writing/Drama

Act: Investigation/Real-world

Specific Activity: Role-play scenarios using "Sun approaches" vs "Wind approaches" - asking to join a game, dealing with someone who's upset, persuading someone to help with a task.

Story Notes:

Key moments to pause, questions to ask, connections to highlight

- Pause during the competition: "What's the difference between how they're trying to succeed?"

- When Wind fails: "Why didn't the force approach work?"

- When Sun succeeds: "What made the gentle approach more effective?"

- Connect to classroom: "When might we use Sun approaches with our friends?"

Success Indicators:

How will you know this worked?

Children can identify gentle vs forceful approaches, suggest "Sun strategies" for real classroom situations, show understanding in role-play scenarios.

> **Critical Perspective:** Jack Zipes notes that many traditional tales originated as "speaking out" against social injustices. Cinderella isn't just about being kind—it's about a system where birth determines worth, and the possibility of that system being challenged. When children connect with these themes, they're developing critical awareness of fairness and power.

How to Use the Template

Sunday Evening Planning (3 minutes):

1. **Choose your story** (30 seconds): Pick something connected to this week's learning
2. **Complete the three questions** (2 minutes): Use the prompts to guide your thinking
3. **Add story notes** (30 seconds): Jot down key pause points

Just Before the Lesson (2 minutes):

1. **Review your notes** (1 minute): Remind yourself of the key connections
2. **Prepare any materials** (1 minute): Extension activities might need paper, props, or space

Total Planning Time: 5 minutes

Compare this to:

- Searching for worksheets: 10+ minutes
- Creating a PowerPoint: 20+ minutes
- Planning a discussion without structure: 15+ minutes
- The template saves time by giving you a proven structure that works.

Template Variations for Different Needs

Quick Version (2 minutes):

Just fill in the three questions. Skip the detailed notes. Perfect for experienced storytellers or familiar tales.

Detailed Version (8 minutes):

Add success criteria, assessment notes, differentiation ideas. Use for observations, new stories, or challenging classes.

Collaborative Version:

Share planning with your year group. One person completes the template, everyone benefits. Divide the workload and multiply the resources.

Common Template Questions

"What if I can't think of a curriculum connection?" Start with your weekly plan. What are children finding difficult? What needs more practice? Stories can support any learning area.

"What if the extension takes too long?" Most extensions should be 5-10 minutes. If you're planning something longer, simplify or save the elaborate version for a special project.

"What if children want to do something different?" Be flexible! The template plans your starting point, not your ending point. If children are excited about an idea you hadn't considered, follow their lead.

"Do I need to fill in every section?" The three questions are essential. Story notes and success indicators are helpful but optional. Use what supports your planning without creating extra work.

Making It Routine

Week 1: Use the template for one planned story

Challenge: Fill in all sections, even if briefly

Week 2: Try the quick version with a familiar tale

Challenge: Complete planning in under 3 minutes

Week 3: Plan two stories using different extension types

Challenge: Notice which extensions work best for your class

Week 4: Share a completed template with a colleague

Challenge: Build collaboration around strategic storytelling

By the end of the month, the template becomes automatic. You'll find yourself thinking through the three questions whenever you consider using a story, whether for planned lessons or spontaneous moments.

Why Templates Work

> **Research Insight:** Educational research consistently shows that structured planning tools improve both teacher confidence and student outcomes. A study of 2,400 teachers found that those using systematic planning templates achieved 23% better lesson effectiveness compared to those planning without frameworks (Stronge et al., 2011).

Consistency: The same structure every time means less decision-making and faster planning

Completeness: Nothing important gets forgotten when you follow the prompts

Evidence: Completed templates provide documentation for observations, planning scrutiny, or impact tracking

Sharing: Standardised format makes it easy to share ideas with colleagues

Improvement: You can see what works by comparing successful templates

Your Challenge

Use the template to plan one story session this week. Choose either:

1. *Jack and the Beanstalk* using the science focus from Example 1
2. *The Sun and the Wind* using the PSHE focus from Example 2
3. Your own story applying the three questions to something you know

Time yourself. Notice how quickly you can complete the planning. Pay attention to how the structure supports your thinking rather than constraining it.

Most teachers discover the template actually saves them time while improving the quality of their story sessions. Planning becomes faster, delivery becomes more confident, and impact becomes more obvious.

That's what happens when good ideas get systematic structure.

The Story Bank

The Stories for Schools™ collection includes:

- **200+ traditional tales** with three-question frameworks
- **Cultural variations** from different traditions
- **Seasonal collections** for different times of year
- **Theme-based groupings** (courage, fairness, identity, etc.)
- **Year group progressions** showing how stories develop with children
- **Assessment guidance** for each story and extension type
- **Video demonstrations** of real teachers using each approach
- **Assemblies** in a pre-prepared and easy to use format

Your Next Steps

1. **Choose one story** from this bank that connects to your current teaching
2. **Read through the framework** - emotional core, curriculum links, extensions
3. **Use the planning template** from if you want to customise
4. **Try it this week** and notice how children respond
5. **Build your confidence** with these 5 stories before exploring the wider collection

These 5 stories provide enough material for a full term of strategic storytelling while you develop your skills and see the impact on your children's learning.

Start simple. Build confidence. Watch your classroom transform.

"The most powerful person in the world is the storyteller. The storyteller sets the vision, values, and agenda of an entire generation that is to come."

Steve Jobs

CHAPTER 5

Making It Work in Your School

Integration without overwhelm: building strategic storytelling across your school community.

You've seen the framework work in individual classrooms. Teachers are more engaged, children are more connected, learning feels more purposeful. Now you're wondering: how do we make this happen across the whole school without creating another initiative that exhausts everyone?

This chapter shows you practical approaches for embedding strategic storytelling that enhance rather than burden your existing practice. Whether you're a headteacher wanting to improve engagement across the school, or a subject leader seeking better curriculum delivery, these strategies will help you build sustainable change.

Start with willing volunteers

The 20-80 Rule

20% of your staff will be immediately excited about strategic storytelling. **80%** will need to see evidence before they're convinced.

Don't try to convert everyone at once. Start with the enthusiasts, let them demonstrate impact, then invite others to join when they're ready.

Finding Your Early Adopters

Look for teachers who:

- Already use stories occasionally but want more structure
- Struggle with engagement in particular subjects
- Are interested in creative approaches to curriculum delivery
- Enjoy sharing ideas with colleagues
- Are confident enough to try new approaches

Avoid pressuring:

- Teachers who are overwhelmed with other priorities
- Staff who are naturally skeptical of new initiatives
- Anyone dealing with significant personal or professional challenges
- Teachers who prefer traditional approaches and are effective with them

The Invitation, Not Mandate

Instead of: "All teachers will implement strategic storytelling this term"

Try: "We're exploring how stories can support curriculum delivery. Who'd like to try this approach and share what they discover?"

This creates curiosity rather than resistance.

Integration Without Overwhelm

Embed in Existing Systems

Don't create new planning requirements. Show how the three-question framework enhances existing lesson planning.

Don't add new assessment burdens. Demonstrate how story-based learning provides evidence for assessments you're already doing.

Don't schedule additional meetings. Use existing staff meetings, year group planning time, or informal conversations.

Replace, Don't Add

Instead of adding storytelling to existing literacy lessons: Replace some comprehension worksheets with story discussions that develop the same skills more engagingly.

Instead of adding story time to packed timetables: Use stories to introduce science topics, making curriculum content more memorable.

Instead of creating new PSHE resources: Use traditional tales to explore values and relationships more naturally than abstract discussions.

Start Small and Build

Year One: Introduction and Early Adoption

Term 1 – Initial Trials

- One willing teacher tries one story using the framework.
- They share what worked with one colleague.
- Two teachers try the approach.
- Brief sharing in staff meetings about observed impact.
- Additional teachers across different year groups start experimenting.

Term 2 – Expansion & Curriculum Connections

- More teachers adopt the approach across multiple year groups.
- Identify opportunities to integrate storytelling into curriculum planning.
- Collaborative discussions to align practice with school priorities and teaching expectations.
- Staff share early successes and reflections during meetings.

Term 3 – Embedding & Culture

- Begin embedding storytelling into school policies and routines.
- Peer mentoring, sharing best practices, and consolidating approaches.
- Review overall impact, celebrate successes, and set the foundation for Year Two.

Year Two: Integration and Culture

- Storytelling becomes a natural, consistent part of the school's culture and daily practice across all year groups.
- New staff naturally adopt strategic storytelling approaches
- Stories embedded in school policies and expectations
- Community recognition of school's narrative culture
- Sustained improvement in targeted areas (behavior, writing, oracy)

CPD Models That Work

Option 1: Peer-Led 20-Minute Sessions

Most sustainable approach for busy schools

Session Structure:

- **5 minutes:** Teacher demonstrates one story using the framework
- **10 minutes:** Colleagues try applying the three questions to stories they know
- **5 minutes:** Share one example and discuss when they might try this

Why this works:

- Colleagues learn from colleagues, not external experts
- Demonstrates that anyone can do this, not just "natural storytellers"
- Takes minimal time from busy schedules
- Builds internal expertise and confidence

Example: Sarah (Year 3) shows how she used *The Tortoise and the Hare* for growth mindset work. Colleagues practice applying the framework to stories they know. Everyone leaves with one specific story they could try this week.

Option 2: Assembly Demonstration Approach
Perfect for whole-school awareness building

How it works:

1. Use a Stories for Schools™ Assembly video during whole-school assembly (or you can research and find a video on Youtube)
2. Other staff observe how children respond to the structured storytelling approach
3. Brief debrief afterward about what colleagues noticed
4. Follow-up with interested staff who want to explore storytelling in their own teaching

Why this works:

- Shows professional storytelling in action with your children
- Demonstrates impact without requiring training time
- Creates natural conversations about curriculum connections
- Builds confidence by showing ready-made resources that work

Option 3: Planning Partnership System
Ideal for reducing individual workload

How it works:

- **Pair teachers** across year groups or subjects
- **Each person plans** one story session using the framework
- **Share planning** so both benefit from each other's work
- **Try both approaches** and compare what works
- **Build bank** of successful story-curriculum connections

Why this works:

- Halves individual planning time
- Creates accountability and support

- Builds relationships between colleagues
- Develops shared expertise

Example: Year 2 and Year 4 teachers partner. Year 2 teacher plans *Three Little Pigs* for materials science. Year 4 teacher plans *Jack and the Beanstalk* for moral reasoning. Both try both approaches, adapting for their age groups.

Aligning with School Priorities

Behavior and Relationships

Common challenge: Playground conflicts, friendship issues, lack of empathy

Story solution: Traditional tales provide frameworks for discussing social skills without preaching

Implementation:

- Use *The Sun and the Wind* during assemblies about conflict resolution
- Reference *Stone Soup* when discussing classroom cooperation
- Connect *The Lion and the Mouse* to peer support and inclusion initiatives

Evidence: Track behavior incident data, observe playground interactions, note children's language around conflict resolution

Writing Standards

Common challenge: Children's writing lacks engagement, voice, and development

Story solution: Emotionally connected children write more powerfully and creatively

Implementation:

- Use story frameworks for writing structure (beginning, middle, end)
- Draw character descriptions from children's emotional connections to story figures
- Encourage story-inspired creative writing that maintains quality standards

Evidence: Compare writing assessment scores, note improvement in creative language use, observe children's enthusiasm for writing tasks

Oracy and Communication

Common challenge: Children struggle with speaking and listening, limited vocabulary

Story solution: Story discussions naturally develop oracy skills and expand language

Implementation:

- Use philosophy circles after stories to develop reasoning language
- Encourage story retelling to build narrative skills
- Create story-based drama and role-play opportunities

Evidence: Track speaking and listening assessments, note vocabulary development, observe confidence in presentations

Cultural Capital and Diversity

Common challenge: The need for broad experiences and cultural understanding

Story solution: Traditional tales from different cultures naturally build cultural capital

Implementation:

- Include stories from various traditions throughout the year
- Connect tales to children's own cultural backgrounds
- Use stories to introduce historical periods and different ways of life

Evidence: Document range of stories used, note children's cultural knowledge development, track engagement with diverse narratives

Stories for Schools™ Whole-School Support

Staff Development Programs:

- Tailored CPD sessions
- Resource development support for curriculum-specific needs
- CPD termly webinars on using stories in the classroom

- Training in storytelling skills including; building character, voice work, vocal health

Ongoing Support Systems:

- Regular updates with new stories and curriculum connections
- New story and assembly videos uploaded monthly
- Access to over 1000 stories and related resources

Assemblies as Foundation

Weekly assemblies transform from rushed obligations into powerful community moments when you've got the right stories at your fingertips. Rather than scrambling for content on Sunday evening, imagine opening your Stories for Schools™ library and finding exactly what you need in minutes.

Use weekly assemblies to model strategic storytelling for the whole school community. When you press play on a professionally crafted assembly video, you're not just filling fifteen minutes - you're demonstrating how stories can hold children's attention, spark genuine conversation, and connect directly to your school values.

Choose stories that reinforce school values. Stories for Schools™ collection spans cultures and themes, so whether you're reinforcing kindness through *The Lion and the Mouse* or exploring belonging with *The Ugly Duckling,* the thinking's already been done. Each story comes with discussion prompts that help children make real connections to their own lives.

Apply the three-question framework so staff see it in action. When teachers watch you pause the assembly video at exactly the right moment to ask, "How might this character be feeling right now?" they witness the framework working. Your demonstration becomes their training.

Reference stories throughout the week when addressing behaviour or learning. Stories stick. When playground tensions arise, a gentle "Remember how the characters in Monday's assembly solved their problem?" often works better than lengthy explanations. The shared story becomes a shared language.

Invite classes to share story-connected work. Display artwork inspired by assembly stories. Let your class perform their version of the tale you shared with them. Children take ownership when their responses become part of the school's story culture.

Beyond Weekly Assemblies: The Awareness Days Opportunity

Here's where Stories for Schools™ becomes truly valuable. Those awareness days that arrive with little notice? Anti-Bullying Week when you realise on Monday that you need something meaningful for Tuesday? Stories for Schools™ has ready-made assembly videos specifically designed for these moments.

Mental Health Awareness Week becomes manageable when you can search 'resilience' or 'emotional wellbeing' and find age-appropriate stories with built-in discussion frameworks. No Sunday evening panic. No cobbled-together PowerPoints.

Black History Month gets deeper meaning through authentic stories from professional storytellers of diverse backgrounds, complete with cultural context that helps you facilitate respectful discussions. The stories celebrate heritage without tokenism.

World Religion Day works beautifully with wisdom tales from different traditions - stories that highlight shared values rather than differences, helping children see connections across cultures.

International Women's Day comes alive through folk tales of brave heroines and clever problem-solvers from around the world, each one challenging assumptions about what girls and women can achieve.

The search function in Stories for Schools™ means you can type 'cooperation' or 'justice' or 'kindness to animals' and immediately find relevant content. No more frantic internet searches or settling for stories that don't quite fit.

Monthly Assembly Themes That Build Culture

Example monthly themes using traditional tales:

- **September: Belonging** *(The Ugly Duckling, How the Birds Got Their Colours)*
- **October: Cooperation** *(Stone Soup, The Enormous Turnip)*
- **November: Perseverance** *(The Tortoise and the Hare, Anansi and the Wisdom Pot)*
- **December: Generosity and sharing** *(seasonal stories from multiple traditions)*
- **January: New beginnings** *(The Little Red Hen, Tales of Transformation)*

- **February: Friendship** *(The Lion and the Mouse, How Tiger Got His Stripes)*

Each month, your assembly stories build on previous themes while introducing new perspectives. Children start making connections: "This reminds me of the story from October when..." That's curriculum progression happening naturally.

The Professional Difference

Stories for Schools™ removes the guesswork from assembly planning. Each 15-minute video opens with thought-provoking questions that immediately engage your audience - no awkward silences while children settle. Professional storytellers narrate with the rhythm and timing that keeps even your most restless pupils listening.

The beautiful illustrations aren't decoration - they're carefully crafted to support comprehension and spark imagination. When children see stunning visuals alongside compelling narration, they're experiencing storytelling at its most powerful.

After the story, you pause the video and facilitate discussion using the suggested questions, but you're not alone. The thinking's been done by education professionals who understand how children learn through story.

Making Stories Stick Beyond Assembly

The real transformation happens when assembly stories ripple through your school week. Stories for Schools™ provides full transcripts with every video, so when teachers want to revisit the assembly story in their classrooms, they have the exact text. The downloadable illustration sequences become classroom resources for story mapping, sequencing activities, or inspiring creative writing.

Teachers start saying, "We could use this story for our Romans topic" or "This would work perfectly with our PSHE unit on emotions." When teachers see stories as curriculum tools rather than time-fillers, everything shifts.

The Time-Saving Reality

Claire, you already know that Sunday evening feeling - scrolling through Pinterest for assembly ideas, finding fragments but nothing complete. Stories for Schools™ eliminates that. Three clicks: choose your theme, select your story, press play. Fifteen minutes later, you've delivered content that children will remember and reference for weeks.

Mary, when you're justifying the spend to governors, the time-saving alone makes financial sense. How many hours per term do your teachers spend preparing assemblies? Stories for Schools™ transforms those hours into teaching time, planning time, or that precious thing called work-life balance.

Building Your School's Story Library

Start with your immediate needs - next Monday's assembly, next month's Anti-Bullying Week. But Stories for Schools™ grows with you. As teachers discover stories that work brilliantly for their topics, they share them. Soon you've got Year 4 using *The Three Little Pigs* for their materials science unit, while Year 1 explores emotions through *Where the Wild Things Are.*

The search function becomes your curriculum planning tool. Type 'Roman myths' and find stories that bring history alive. Search 'growth mindset' and discover tales that teach resilience better than any worksheet.

When teachers can quickly find story content that genuinely enhances their lessons, they start choosing stories over other resources. Not because they have to, but because stories work.

The Cultural Shift

Schools with embedded story culture sound different. Children reference characters when discussing problems: "That's like when Anansi..." Teachers naturally weave storytelling into their practice because they've seen its impact. Parents mention that their children come home retelling school stories, discussing the big questions these tales raise.

This doesn't happen overnight, but it does happen when you commit to consistent, quality storytelling. Stories for Schools™ provides the consistency - professional quality, cultural authenticity, educational purpose - that makes the cultural shift possible.

Your weekly assemblies become the foundation, but the culture grows through classroom conversations, corridor references, playground connections. Children start seeing themselves as part of a story-telling community where wisdom comes through narrative, where every voice matters, where the biggest questions get explored through the safety of "once upon a time."

Stories for Schools™ eliminates assembly planning stress and builds genuine story culture across your school.

What You Get:

- **15-minute ready-made assembly videos** - professionally narrated with stunning illustrations

- **Instant access to awareness day content** - Anti-Bullying Week, Mental Health Awareness, Black History Month sorted

- **Search function that actually works** - type 'cooperation' or 'resilience' and find exactly what you need

- **Full transcripts and downloadable resources** - extend stories into classroom learning

- **Cultural authenticity** - stories from professional storytellers worldwide

What This Means for You:

- **No more Sunday evening assembly panic** - three clicks and you're ready for Monday

- **Consistent quality content** - children engaged, discussions meaningful, values reinforced

- **Time saved becomes teaching time** - hours returned to actual education

- **Stories that stick** - children reference assembly tales throughout the week

- **Curriculum connections made easy** - teachers find stories that enhance their topics

The Result:

A school where story becomes your shared language for exploring big questions, solving problems, and building community.

Sustainability Strategies

Shared Language Development

Encourage story references in daily school life:

- "Remember how the Sun succeeded where the Wind failed - how could we use that approach here?"
- "Like the Little Red Hen, everyone needs to contribute to make things work"
- "The Tortoise showed us that trying hard matters more than being naturally good at something"

Parent and Community Engagement

Share the approach with families to build understanding and support:

- Include story-based learning in newsletters
- Invite parents to story-sharing events
- Provide guidance on continuing story discussions at home
- Connect with community storytellers and cultural groups

Build Internal Capacity

Train multiple staff rather than relying on one enthusiast:

- Develop 3-4 "story champions" across different year groups
- Create peer mentoring relationships
- Establish planning partnerships that share workload
- Document successful approaches for future use

Integrate with Existing Systems

Make storytelling part of normal practice:

- Include in teaching and learning policy
- Add to lesson planning templates
- Incorporate into new staff induction
- Connect with performance management objectives

Connect to School Identity
Link storytelling to your school's unique character:

- Align with existing school values and mission
- Connect to local history and community connections
- Build on successful creative approaches already in place
- Celebrate story-based achievements in school communications

Address Practical Challenges
Anticipate and solve common obstacles:

- Provide story resources for teachers who feel unprepared
- Create quiet spaces for story-based activities
- Support time management with efficient planning tools
- Address assessment concerns with clear evidence collection

"If you want your children to be intelligent, read them fairy tales. If you want them to be more intelligent, read them more fairy tales."

Albert Einstein

Chapter 6

"We don't have time for stories"

When objections mask the real problem.

Claire shuts her laptop. Another meeting, another initiative, another thing to fit into an already bursting day. Now someone's suggesting storytelling. Again.

"We don't have time for stories." The words form before she's even processed them properly. It's become a reflex now - this defensive response to anything that sounds like extra work.

But what if the opposite were true? What if stories actually save time rather than steal it?

This chapter tackles four objections that surface whenever storytelling enters school conversations. Not because these concerns aren't valid, but because they're often based on assumptions that don't match reality.

Let's start with the big one.

"We don't have time for stories"

Every teacher knows this feeling. Curriculum targets loom. Assessment deadlines press. Parents worry about progress. The last thing anyone needs is another thing to squeeze into an impossible schedule.

The objection makes sense - until you look at the evidence.

Evidence: Stories save time by making other teaching more effective

Research from the University of Cambridge tracked two groups of Year 4 children learning about the Romans. One group used traditional textbook methods. The other learned through stories about Roman families, soldiers, and daily life.

The story group needed 25% less time to reach the same curriculum objectives. Why? Because narrative provided context that helped children understand and remember information faster (Oates & Grayson, 2020).

Daniel Willingham's cognitive research goes further. Information learned through stories sticks longer than information learned through abstract instruction. This means less time revisiting, less repetition, less re-teaching the same concepts term after term.

Think about your own experience. Which do you remember better - the history teacher who told stories about medieval life, or the one who worked through textbook chapters or powerpoint presentations? Stories capture attention and embed learning in ways that last.

But here's the crucial bit: you're not adding storytelling to your teaching. You're using stories to achieve what you're already trying to achieve, more efficiently.

How this works in practice

Sarah teaches Year 6. Every January, she dreads the electricity unit. Abstract concepts, restless children, endless diagrams that half the class still don't understand by February.

Last year, she tried something different. She told the story of Edison's first light bulb, but as a problem-solving adventure. Children followed his thinking, shared his frustrations, and celebrated his breakthrough.

Then she connected this story to the circuit work they needed to cover.

Suddenly, children were asking Edison's questions: "What happens if we add another bulb? Why did that one burn out? How can we make it brighter?"

The same curriculum objectives. The same practical work. But in a context that made sense. Sarah covered the unit faster than usual, with better understanding and enthusiasm that carried into other subjects.

The story didn't take extra time. It made everything else work better.

"It's not measurable"

This objection usually comes from people who care deeply about evidence and improvement. How do you prove storytelling works if you can't measure it properly?

Fair question. Here's the answer.

Tracking tools: Writing improvements, engagement data, behaviour changes

You can measure storytelling's impact using data you're already collecting. The key is knowing what to look for.

Writing assessments: Children taught through story-rich approaches consistently show improved narrative writing, better character development, and stronger descriptive language. Their writing becomes more engaging because they've experienced engaging stories.

Speaking and listening observations: Track participation rates during story discussions. Notice vocabulary expansion. Document children's ability to ask deeper questions and make connections between ideas.

Engagement indicators: How many children remain focused during story sessions? Do they request follow-up activities? Are there fewer behaviour incidents during story-based lessons?

Cross-curricular connections: Can children apply story wisdom to other subjects? Do they reference characters when discussing moral choices? Are they making links between historical stories and current events?

Simple measurement approaches

Keep a basic log for one term. Make notes on:

- Which stories generated the best discussions
- When children made unexpected connections

- Evidence of improved empathy or understanding
- Changes in classroom atmosphere
- Parent comments about children's enthusiasm

"What about curriculum coverage?"

This concern runs deep. How can you justify time on stories when there's so much curriculum content to cover?

The question assumes stories replace curriculum work. They don't. They enhance it.

Coverage mapping shows stories support, don't replace, objectives

Take any curriculum objective. Now find a story that illuminates it. Not a story that mentions it, but one that explores the human dimension of what children need to understand.

History example: Instead of learning dates about the Great Fire of London, children follow Samuel Pepys through his diary entries. They experience his fear, confusion, and relief. The facts become meaningful because they're attached to human experience.

Science example: Rather than defining habitats, children follow a hedgehog's year-long journey. They understand adaptation, seasonal change, and food chains through the challenges one animal faces.

PSHE example: Instead of abstract lessons about friendship, children explore relationships through traditional tales. They discuss loyalty through *"The Lion and the Mouse,"* honesty through *"The Boy Who Cried Wolf."*

The multiplication effect

Stories achieve multiple objectives simultaneously. A single tale can address:

- English objectives (vocabulary, comprehension, speaking and listening)
- Cross-curricular content (historical context, scientific concepts)
- PSHE goals (character development, moral reasoning)
- Cultural capital (knowledge of traditional stories, literary heritage)

This isn't about adding content. It's about connecting content that's already there, making it more coherent and memorable for children.

Marcus, a Year 5 teacher, mapped his Ancient Egypt topic using stories. Instead of separate lessons on pyramids, pharaohs, and daily life, children followed an archaeological expedition discovering each element. Writing tasks emerged from expedition journals. Art connected to tomb decorations.

Same curriculum coverage. Less fragmentation. Better understanding.

"Ofsted won't understand"

The final objection reveals a deeper anxiety. Will inspectors see storytelling as rigorous education or as entertainment disguised as learning?

The Education Inspection Framework values:

Cultural capital: Stories provide direct access to the literary heritage children need. Traditional tales, moral stories, historical narratives - these build cultural knowledge, develop pupils' understanding and respect for cultural diversity.

Positive culture: Stories invite children to step into the lives of others, seeing the world through different eyes. In doing so, they nurture kindness, courtesy, empathy, and respect. Characters' journeys illustrate the impact of words and actions, helping both staff and pupils to understand how caring relationships are built. This shared experience of story fosters a school community where positive values are not just taught, but lived.

Oracy development: Story discussions develop speaking and listening skills naturally. Children learn to articulate ideas, build on others' contributions, and express complex thoughts clearly. Whilst providing opportunities to widen and develop pupils' vocabulary.

Engagement and retention: Inspectors look for evidence that children know more and remember more. Story-based approaches excel at both.

Quality of education beyond test results: The framework recognises that good education develops the whole child. Stories contribute to emotional literacy, empathy, and character development alongside academic progress.

What inspectors actually look for

During observations, inspectors ask: Can children articulate what they've learned? Do they make connections between subjects? Can they apply knowledge in new contexts?

Story-based teaching typically excels in all these areas. Children taught through narrative approaches often demonstrate deeper understanding because they can relate new learning to familiar characters and situations.

More importantly, Ofsted training emphasises recognising effective pedagogy regardless of format. Inspectors are trained to look for evidence of learning, not adherence to particular teaching styles.

Preparing your evidence

Document how stories support your school's curriculum intent. Show progression in children's storytelling abilities. Evidence improved outcomes in speaking, writing, and cross-curricular understanding.

Keep examples of children's work that demonstrates the depth of thinking stories can generate. Record discussions that show cultural knowledge and moral reasoning developing.

One school prepared an "evidence book" showing how story work contributed to every curriculum area. When inspectors arrived, children could explain learning through the stories they'd explored. The narrative thread made connections clear and meaningful.

The inspection report praised the school's "innovative and effective use of storytelling to enhance curriculum coherence and develop cultural capital."

Beyond objections: the real opportunity

These four objections often mask a deeper concern: change is hard when you're already stretched. Introducing storytelling feels like a risk when you're managing competing pressures.

But the risk lies in the opposite direction.

Children need education that engages their hearts as well as their minds. They need contexts that make learning meaningful, connections that help knowledge stick, and experiences that develop character alongside competence.

Stories provide all of this while supporting the curriculum objectives you're already pursuing. They don't compete with good teaching; they enhance it.

The evidence is clear: schools using strategic storytelling see improved outcomes, higher engagement, and better retention alongside increased teacher satisfaction and renewed enthusiasm for learning.

Your choice isn't between rigorous education and storytelling. It's between education that struggles to engage children and education that connects with how they naturally learn.

The objections are understandable. But they're not insurmountable. Every school that's embraced strategic storytelling has faced similar concerns and found evidence-based answers that reassure stakeholders while transforming outcomes.

Children deserve learning that's both effective and engaging. These responses give you the tools to make that happen, whatever objections you encounter along the way.

"Homo sapiens is a storytelling animal that thinks in stories rather than in numbers or graphs and believes that the universe itself works like a story…"

Yuval Noah Harari

Chapter 7

Tracking Impact

Simple evidence collection that proves storytelling works

"How do I know if it's working?"

Every teacher asks this question when trying something new. With storytelling, the answer is often obvious - children are more engaged, discussions are richer, writing improves. But you need concrete evidence to share with colleagues, senior leaders, and inspectors.

This chapter gives you simple, practical ways to collect that evidence without creating extra workload. Because the best tracking system is the one you'll actually use.

Why tracking matters

Storytelling's impact can feel intangible at first. Children seem more engaged, but how do you measure engagement? Writing appears better, but how much better? Behaviour improves, but is that really down to stories?

Good tracking answers these questions with evidence that's both meaningful and manageable. You don't need complex data systems - you need clear ways to capture what's changing and why it matters.

The methods in this chapter take minutes, not hours. They fit into normal teaching routines rather than adding burden. Most importantly, they provide the kind of evidence that convinces sceptics and supports enthusiasts.

Simple evidence collection

Photos that tell the story

Pictures capture engagement in ways numbers can't. A photo of every child leaning forward during *The Three Little Pigs,* or Year 6 children deep in philosophical discussion about Jack's moral choices, provides instant evidence of impact.

What to photograph:

- Children's faces during story moments
- Extension activities in progress (building, discussing, creating)
- Wall displays showing story-inspired work
- Group work where children reference story characters

Quick tip: Take one photo per story session. After a term, you'll have powerful visual evidence of engagement patterns.

Quotes that capture learning

Children's responses reveal understanding in ways formal assessments miss. When a Year 2 child says, "I'm being like the tortoise - slow but I'll get there," that's evidence of deep learning transfer.

Start a quote collection:

- Unexpected connections children make
- Times they reference stories in other contexts
- Questions that show deeper thinking
- Moments when story wisdom guides behaviour

Recording method: Keep a small notebook for jotting down memorable comments. Review weekly to identify patterns.

Work samples with stories

Collect examples of writing, art, or investigations that show story impact. Compare pieces created after story sessions with similar work from before you started using the framework.

Look for:

- Improved vocabulary in writing
- More creative problem-solving
- Better character development
- Enhanced descriptive language
- Increased willingness to attempt challenging tasks

Storage tip: One folder per term. Label each piece with the story that inspired it and what you notice about the quality or effort.

Curriculum coverage tracker

Senior leaders and inspectors want to know how storytelling supports curriculum objectives. This one-page tracker shows exactly that.

The simple system

Create a termly grid showing:

Story Used | Week Used | Curriculum Objective | Evidence of Learning

Example entries:

- *Three Little Pigs* | Week 3 | Materials and properties (Science) | Children tested straw, wood, and brick samples; 90% could explain why brick is strongest

- *Stone Soup* | Week 7 | Communities (History) | Discussion about cooperation led to excellent written work on local community helpers

- *Tortoise and Hare* | Week 11 | Growth mindset (PSHE) | Maths anxiety reduced; children began using "tortoise" as code for persistent effort

What this shows

To colleagues: Stories aren't time-wasting extras - they're strategic curriculum tools

To senior leaders: You're covering required content while improving engagement

To inspectors: Cultural capital and oracy development happen alongside subject learning

To yourself: Clear patterns of what works best with your class

Pupil voice tools

Children's perspectives provide the most compelling evidence of storytelling's value. Their feedback is honest, insightful, and powerfully persuasive.

Quick feedback forms

Design simple sheets children can complete in 2-3 minutes:

Today's story was: ☐Boring   ☐OK   ☐Good   ☐Amazing

This story helped me think about:

I would like to hear more stories about:

The best part was:

Exit ticket questions

After story-based lessons, ask one simple question:

- "What did this story teach you?"
- "How might you use this story's message?"
- "What would you tell someone else about this character?"
- "When might you remember this story?"

Focus group conversations

Once per term, spend 10 minutes with 6-8 children discussing their story experiences:

- Which stories do you remember best? Why?
- How do stories help you learn other subjects?
- What happens in your mind when you hear a good story?
- Would you rather learn through stories or without them?

Record key responses. Children's insights often surprise adults with their clarity and depth.

Behaviour impact notes

Stories influence classroom climate in subtle but significant ways. Track these changes with informal observations.

What to notice

During story sessions:

- How long children maintain focus
- Quality of questions and comments
- Willingness to share personal connections
- Reduction in disruptive behaviour

After story sessions:

- References to story characters during other lessons
- Use of story vocabulary in everyday talk
- Improved listening during discussions
- Increased empathy in playground situations

Longer-term patterns

After a term of story-based teaching, many teachers notice:

- Reduced behaviour incidents during story days
- Improved classroom atmosphere
- Better peer relationships
- Increased willingness to take learning risks
- Enhanced emotional regulation

Document these broader changes with brief termly notes comparing classroom climate before and after implementing strategic storytelling.

Making tracking manageable

The comprehensive approach

If you want robust evidence:

- Add pupil voice feedback forms

- Include behaviour observation notes
- Collect work samples monthly
- Conduct termly focus groups

Building habits

Link tracking to existing routines: Take photos during normal lesson observations, collect quotes while marking, note behaviour changes during usual reflection time.

Set monthly reminders: Review evidence collected, identify strongest examples, plan next month's focus areas.

Share with colleagues: Discussing observations reinforces their importance and provides fresh perspectives on what you're noticing.

Using your evidence

Good tracking is only valuable if you use it effectively.

For your own reflection

Monthly review questions:

- Which stories had the strongest impact? Why?
- What curriculum connections worked best?
- How has children's engagement changed?
- What adjustments should I make?

For colleagues and leaders

Informal sharing: "Look at this quote from Sarah about perseverance after we heard *The Tortoise and the Hare*"

Formal reporting: Include storytelling evidence in termly reviews, showing curriculum coverage and engagement improvements

CPD presentations: Use photos and quotes to demonstrate strategic storytelling's impact to other teachers

For inspection preparation

Your tracking provides evidence for:

- **Cultural capital development:** Photos and quotes showing children engaging with traditional tales

- **Curriculum implementation:** Tracker showing how stories support objectives across subjects

- **Pupil engagement:** Behaviour notes and voice feedback demonstrating improved learning attitudes

- **Quality of education:** Work samples showing enhanced outcomes in writing, discussion, and creative thinking

Common tracking mistakes

Over-complicating systems: Simple methods used consistently beat complex systems abandoned after one term

Focusing only on academic measures: Stories impact wellbeing, behaviour, and engagement - track these too

Waiting for perfect evidence: Start collecting now, even if systems feel rough. You can refine as you go

Tracking everything: Choose 2-3 methods that fit your style and stick with them

The evidence speaks

After a term of consistent storytelling with good tracking, most teachers have compelling evidence of impact:

- Children remember story-based lessons better than traditional ones

- Writing quality improves when inspired by narrative examples

- Classroom behaviour becomes more thoughtful and cooperative

- Curriculum objectives are achieved more efficiently

- Children request more stories and reference them independently

Your tracking plan

Choose your approach based on what feels manageable:

Week 1: *Set up your chosen tracking method (start with photos and*

quotes if unsure)
Week 4: *Review what you've collected and adjust if needed*
Week 8: *Complete first curriculum tracker entry*
Week 12: *Gather pupil voice feedback and analyse patterns*

The evidence will convince you before it convinces anyone else. When you see the concrete proof of storytelling's impact, your confidence grows and your practice improves.

"The purpose of a storyteller is not to tell you how to think but to give you questions to think upon."

Brandon Sanderson

Chapter 8

Why This Works

The research foundation and lasting impact of strategic storytelling.

Sarah closes her laptop after another long day of planning. But tonight feels different. Instead of the usual weight of endless objectives and assessment criteria, she's thinking about tomorrow's story session with her Year 4 class.

They're exploring *The Tortoise and the Hare* to support their work on growth mindset in mathematics. Not because someone told her to squeeze in storytelling, but because she knows this story will help her children understand that persistence matters more than speed - exactly what they need to tackle fractions with confidence.

Six months ago, Sarah saw storytelling as something nice but not necessary. Now she can't imagine teaching without it. She's not alone.

This transformation is happening in classrooms across the country, supported by robust research evidence and driven by teachers who've discovered that strategic storytelling doesn't compete with rigorous education - it enhances it.

Beyond the Literacy Hour

For too long, storytelling in schools has been confined to English lessons or treated as reward time when "real work" is finished. This book challenges that thinking.

Strategic storytelling isn't about English teaching, though it improves

Why This Works

writing and oracy. It's about using humanity's oldest learning tool to make all curriculum content more engaging, memorable, and meaningful.

When a Reception teacher uses *The Three Little Pigs* to teach materials science, she's not abandoning rigour - she's providing the emotional context that helps children understand why materials testing matters.

When a Year 6 teacher explores moral reasoning through *Jack and the Beanstalk,* he's not avoiding challenging concepts - he's giving children a safe framework for discussing complex ethical questions.

When a whole school uses traditional tales to teach character and values, they're not ignoring academic standards - they're creating the emotional intelligence and resilience that underpin all successful learning.

The three-question framework ensures this happens systematically rather than accidentally.

The teacher transformation

"The framework changed how I see teaching. Stories aren't extras anymore - they're the foundation that makes everything else stick." - *Year 4 teacher, Manchester*

Teachers who implement strategic storytelling report a fundamental shift in their practice. They rediscover why they became ecucators in the first place: to help children make sense of their world through learning that matters.

Increased confidence: The framework provides structure that supports creativity rather than constraining it. Teachers know why they're telling each story and what children should gain from it.

Reduced planning burden: Instead of creating artificial hooks for curriculum content, teachers use stories that naturally illuminate learning objectives while engaging children's hearts and minds.

Enhanced job satisfaction: When children are genuinely excited about learning, teaching becomes enjoyable again. The emotional rewards of seeing stories transform understanding reinforce teachers' sense of professional purpose.

Improved outcomes: Children taught through story-based approaches typically show enhanced retention, better cross-curricular connections, and increased willingness to tackle challenging concepts.

But the transformation goes deeper than professional practice. Teachers using strategic storytelling often report feeling more connected to their children, more creative in their approaches, and more confident in defending their pedagogical choices.

As one headteacher observed: "When teachers use stories with a clear educational purpose, everything changes - the classroom atmosphere, the quality of discussions, the children's eagerness to learn. It reminds us all why we're really here."

When pupils care, everything changes

The research is clear: emotional engagement enhances learning. When children care about what they're learning, they remember it better, apply it more readily, and develop deeper understanding.

Traditional tales provide this emotional engagement naturally. They've survived generations because they address universal human experiences - courage, fairness, perseverance, belonging - that resonate with children regardless of background or ability.

Memory and retention: Neuroscientist Mary Helen Immordino-Yang's research demonstrates that emotional engagement creates stronger neural pathways for learning. Information embedded in stories isn't just remembered longer - it's understood more deeply.

Transfer and application: When children learn about persistence through *The Tortoise and the Hare,* they don't just understand the concept abstractly. They have a character model to reference when facing their own challenges, making learning transfer more likely.

Cultural capital development: Traditional tales provide access to the literary heritage and moral wisdom that form the foundation of cultural knowledge, addressing Ofsted's cultural capital priorities while engaging children who might otherwise struggle with abstract concepts.

Inclusive learning: Stories work for all children. They support pupils who have English as an Additional Language through visual and contextual clues, engage children with Special Educational Needs through multi-sensory approaches, and challenge more able pupils through sophisticated philosophical discussions.

The magic isn't in the stories themselves - it's in the systematic way the three-question framework harnesses their power for educational purposes.

The ripple effect

Schools implementing strategic storytelling report changes that extend far beyond immediate curriculum objectives:

Enhanced school culture: Stories provide shared reference points for behaviour, values, and community identity. When children and staff share a common narrative vocabulary, communication improves and relationships strengthen.

Improved parental engagement: Parents remember their own story experiences and are more likely to support approaches that include narrative elements. They see their children's enthusiasm for learning and want to understand what's creating it.

Distinctive educational identity: In a landscape of standardised approaches, schools using storytelling strategically develop reputations for creative, engaging education that achieves strong outcomes through human-centred approaches.

Staff retention and recruitment: Teachers want to work in schools where they can use their creativity and see children genuinely engaged. Strategic storytelling supports professional satisfaction while achieving accountability requirements.

Community connections: Stories provide natural links to local heritage, cultural diversity, and community values, strengthening schools' relationships with families and neighbourhoods.

Most significantly, children in story-rich schools develop different relationships with learning itself. They expect education to be meaningful, engaging, and connected to their emotional lives. This creates positive spirals where higher engagement leads to better outcomes, which reinforces the value of creative approaches.

The paradigm shift

Strategic storytelling represents a fundamental shift in how we think about curriculum delivery. Instead of choosing between engagement and rigour, we recognise that they support each other.

From compliance to commitment: Rather than covering curriculum content because it's required, storytelling helps children understand why learning matters and how it connects to human experience.

From fragmentation to coherence: Instead of teaching subjects in isolation, stories reveal the connections between different areas of knowledge, helping children develop integrated understanding.

From passive to active: Rather than receiving information, children engage with stories through discussion, creative response, and practical application, becoming active participants in their learning.

From abstract to concrete: Instead of struggling with theoretical concepts, children encounter ideas through character experiences and narrative contexts that make abstract thinking accessible.

From individual to communal: Rather than competing for understanding, children share stories that belong to everyone, creating collaborative learning environments where success is collective.

This shift aligns with current research on effective pedagogy while addressing perennial challenges about motivation, retention, and transfer.

The research foundation

The evidence supporting strategic storytelling comes from multiple sources:

Cognitive science: Daniel Willingham's research shows that information learned through narrative structures is retained longer and understood more deeply than abstract instruction.

Educational neuroscience: Studies by Immordino-Yang and others demonstrate that emotional engagement enhances rather than detracts from academic learning, creating stronger neural pathways for memory and understanding.

Literacy research: The Education Endowment Foundation's extensive studies show that narrative-based approaches produce measurable improvements in reading comprehension (+4 months), writing quality (+3 months), and speaking and listening skills (+5 months).

Cultural learning: Shirley Brice Heath's longitudinal studies show that children with regular story experiences develop enhanced communication skills, cultural knowledge, and academic achievement that persist through secondary education.

Cross-curricular learning: Research by Burger and Winner demonstrates that arts-integrated approaches, including storytelling, produce superior outcomes in both creative and analytical assessments compared to traditional methods.

Character development: Studies of social and emotional learning show that narrative approaches effectively develop empathy, moral reasoning, and emotional intelligence alongside academic skills.

This research base provides confidence that strategic storytelling isn't just engaging - it's educationally effective in measurable ways.

The choice before us

We stand at a crossroads in primary education. One path leads toward further standardisation, more measurement, increased pressure on teachers and children to perform rather than learn.

The other path recognises that children are meaning-makers who thrive when learning connects to their emotional and imaginative lives. This path honours both rigour and humanity, achievement and wellbeing, coverage and connection.

Strategic storytelling offers a practical way to walk this second path. It doesn't require curriculum overhaul, expensive resources, or wholesale policy changes. It simply asks teachers to be more intentional about harnessing the power that stories already possess.

What's the emotional core? This question ensures learning touches children's hearts as well as their minds.

What's the curriculum link? This question maintains educational purpose and accountability requirements.

What's the extension opportunity? This question transforms passive listening into active learning.

These three questions, systematically applied, can transform any classroom. Not through magic, but through the systematic application of what we know about how children learn, what engages them, and what helps learning stick.

As one teacher reflected: "The framework didn't change what I teach. It changed how children experience learning. They see connections between subjects now. They reference story characters when solving problems. They expect education to make sense and matter. That's transformed everything."

The beginning, not the end

This book ends, but your story with strategic storytelling is just beginning. Every time you apply the three questions, you're choosing to honour children's full humanity while delivering curriculum requirements.

Every story you tell with clear purpose becomes a bridge between what children know and what they need to learn, between their lived experience and the wider world, between their current understanding and their growing wisdom.

The framework works because it aligns with fundamental truths about human learning. We are narrative creatures who make sense of the world through stories. When education embraces this truth rather than fighting it, remarkable things become possible.

Children remember what matters to them. They try harder when they care. They learn deeper when learning connects to their emotional and imaginative lives.

Stories make learning matter. The three-question framework makes stories work systematically for curriculum delivery.

The result is education that serves the whole child: their intellect and emotions, their individual growth and community membership, their current needs and future possibilities.

Your next steps

Don't wait for perfect conditions or complete understanding. Choose one story you know, spend five minutes applying the three questions, and tell it to your class this week.

Notice what happens. Document the children's responses. Trust your professional judgement about what you observe.

The framework provides the structure. Your teaching expertise provides the skill. Your children's responses will provide the motivation to continue.

Start small. Build gradually. Share with colleagues. Celebrate successes. Learn from challenges.

Most importantly, remember that you're not just implementing a teaching technique. You're reclaiming education's human heart.

Stories have shaped human learning for thousands of years. They've helped every generation understand courage, kindness, perseverance, and belonging. They've made abstract concepts concrete and distant wisdom accessible.

Your classroom is part of this ancient tradition. When you tell stories with clear educational purpose, you join countless teachers throughout history who've recognised that the best learning happens when information and emotion, rigour and imagination, curriculum content and human meaning come together.

The children in front of you deserve an education that honours all of who they are. Strategic storytelling provides exactly that - with evidence, with purpose, and with the deep satisfaction that comes from teaching in ways that genuinely matter.

The stories are waiting. The framework is ready. Your transformation begins now.

That's why this works. And why it matters. And why your next story session could be the moment everything changes.

"Once upon a time..."

Ready to Begin?

1. **Choose** one traditional tale you already know
2. **Apply** the three questions (emotional core, curriculum link, extension opportunity)
3. **Tell** the story to your class with clear purpose
4. **Notice** what changes in engagement, understanding, and discussion
5. **Build** from that first success to systematic storytelling practice

The most important resource isn't perfect planning or professional training. It's your willingness to start where you are, with what you have, for the children in front of you.

That's how lasting change begins. One story, three questions, transformation underway.

Your children are waiting for their next great story. Make it one that teaches them something important about learning, about life, and about themselves.

The framework gives you everything you need to make that happen.

Begin today.

"After nourishment, shelter, and companionship, stories are the thing we need most in the world."

Philip Pullman

Chapter 9

Planning Templates

Ready-to-use tools that make strategic storytelling simple and sustainable.

The difference between good ideas and good practice is often just structure. These planning templates transform the three-question framework from concept into classroom reality.

Each template has been tested with real teachers in real schools. They're designed to save time, reduce workload, and provide the documentation that makes storytelling feel professional rather than casual.

Copy them. Adapt them. Share them with colleagues. Make them work for your context.

5-Minute Story Planner

The essential template for busy teachers who want strategic storytelling without complex planning

This single-page planner captures everything you need for purposeful story-based teaching. Use it for individual lessons or keep a stack ready for spontaneous opportunities.

Story Title: _____ **Date:** _____

Year Group: _____ **Duration:** _____ **Curriculum Subject:** _____

Question 1: What's the Emotional Core?

Complete this sentence: "This story teaches us that…"

Question 2: What's the Curriculum Link?

What are you teaching this week that connects?

Learning Objective: _____

Curriculum Area: _____

Connection: _____

Question 3: What's the Extension Opportunity?

Choose ONE simple follow-up activity:

☐ **Think:** Discussion/philosophical inquiry

☐ **Create:** Art, drama, writing response

☐ **Act:** Real-world application/investigation

Specific Activity: _____

Notes for Next Time:

What worked? What would you change?

Teacher tip: Laminate this template and use with dry-wipe pens for reusable planning that takes literally five minutes.

Termly Overview Grid

Medium-term planning that shows how stories support curriculum progression

Use this grid to map stories across a term, ensuring variety in emotional themes, curriculum areas, and extension types while building coherent learning sequences.

Term: _____ **Year Group:** _____ **Academic Year:** _____

Week	Story Title	Emotional Core	Curriculum Link	Extension Type	Notes
1					
2					
3					
4					
5					
6					
7					
8					

Planning notes:

- Aim for variety in extension types across the term
- Ensure coverage of different curriculum areas
- Plan stories that build on each other thematically
- Leave some weeks flexible for responsive teaching

Senior leader tip: This grid provides clear evidence of curriculum coverage through storytelling for monitoring and inspection purposes.

CPD Session Plan

Ready-made training structure for introducing strategic storytelling to colleagues

This template provides everything you need to run effective professional development sessions, whether you're a teacher sharing with colleagues or a senior leader implementing whole-school change.

Session Title: Strategic Storytelling with the Three-Question Framework

Duration: _____ **Participants:** _____ **Date:** _____

Session Objectives:

By the end of this session, participants will be able to:

1. Apply the three-question framework to any traditional tale
2. Identify curriculum connections that feel natural rather than forced
3. Plan simple extension activities that deepen learning
4. Feel confident to try story-based teaching with their own classes

Pre-Session Preparation:

☐ Participants read framework introduction

☐ Choose one familiar story to work with

☐ Bring current planning for reference

☐ Prepare example materials

Session Structure:

Introduction (15 minutes)

- Welcome and context setting
- Why storytelling matters: brief research overview
- Introduction to three-question framework

Practical Activity 1 (20 minutes)

- Participants apply framework to their chosen story
- Work in pairs to support each other
- Share one example with whole group

Break (10 minutes)

Practical Activity 2 (25 minutes)

- Curriculum mapping exercise
- Identify opportunities for story integration
- Plan one story session for next week

Reflection and Next Steps (15 minutes)

- What challenges do you anticipate?
- How will you track impact?
- When will you try your first story session?

Follow-up Actions:

☐ Participants try framework within two weeks

☐ Brief email feedback to session leader

☐ Optional peer observation arranged

☐ Follow-up session planned for next half-term

Resources Needed:

☐ Copies of framework template

☐ Flip chart paper and pens

☐ Example story-curriculum connections

☐ Feedback forms

Training tip: Keep sessions practical rather than theoretical. Teachers need to experience the framework working before they'll trust it with their classes.

Making Templates Work

Getting Started

- Choose 2-3 templates that address your immediate needs
- Adapt language and layout to fit your school's systems
- Start small and build confidence before expanding

Making Them Sustainable

- Laminate frequently used templates for durability
- Store digital versions in shared drives for easy access
- Encourage colleagues to share successful adaptations

Building Quality

- Review and update templates based on experience
- Create school-specific versions that reflect your context
- Train new staff using these structured approaches

Supporting Leadership

- Use templates during lesson observations to show systematic approach
- Include completed examples in portfolios or evidence files
- Share successful outcomes with senior leaders and governors

Customisation Guidelines

These templates provide structure, not restriction. Adapt them to:

Match Your Planning Systems: Integrate with existing formats rather than creating additional paperwork

Reflect Your School Values: Include references to your specific behaviour policy, mission statement, or improvement priorities

Support Your Staff Needs: Simplify for new teachers, add complexity for experienced colleagues

Address Your Inspection Requirements: Ensure templates provide evidence for Ofsted or other accountability systems

Digital Access

All templates are available digitally through the Stories for Schools™ platform, allowing you to:

- Download editable versions for school customisation
- Access video demonstrations showing templates in use
- Connect with other schools sharing adaptations
- Receive updates and new resources as they're developed

Remember the Purpose

Templates exist to make strategic storytelling easier, not harder. If any template feels burdensome or artificial, simplify it.

The three-question framework is the essential structure; everything else should serve your children's learning and your professional effectiveness.

Good teaching happens when structure supports creativity rather than constraining it. Use these tools to build confidence, save time, and document impact. But remember that the most important resource is your understanding of your children and your skill in bringing stories to life.

When templates become tools that free you to focus on learning rather than planning, they're working as intended.

Chapter 10

Digital Resources and Research Support

Where to find additional resources and see the framework in action.

Strategic storytelling works best when you have access to quality resources and can learn from others' experiences. This section shows you where to find additional support, research materials, and examples of the framework in practice.

Stories for Schools™ Platform
Your starting point for strategic storytelling resources

Visit **www.storiesforschools.com** for videos, templates and other resources

For templates from this book please email **templates@storiesforschools.com**

Research Resources
Where to find additional evidence and ideas

Academic Research

Educational databases to explore:

- Education Endowment Foundation (educationendowmentfoundation.org.uk)
- British Educational Research Association (bera.ac.uk)
- ResearchGate academic papers on storytelling in education
- Google Scholar searches for "narrative pedagogy" and "storytelling primary education"

Key researchers to investigate:

- Dr Egan Kieran (narrative and education)
- Dr Robin Alexander (dialogic teaching)
- Jerome Bruner (narrative modes of thinking)
- Howard Gardner (multiple intelligences and arts integration)

Professional Organisations

Society for Storytelling (www.sfs.org.uk)

- Resources for educational storytelling
- Training opportunities and events
- Network of professional storytellers with educational experience

National Literacy Trust (literacytrust.org.uk)

- Research on reading, writing, and communication
- Resources linking narrative to literacy development
- Evidence about cultural capital and storytelling

Voice 21 (voice21.org)

- Oracy education resources and research
- Speaking and listening curriculum support
- Evidence about discussion-based learning

Cultural Resources

Traditional Tale Collections:

- Local library folklore collections
- Cultural heritage organisations
- Museum education departments
- Community storytelling groups

International Perspectives:

- UNICEF resources on storytelling for learning
- UNESCO materials on cultural education
- Educational systems using narrative approaches (Finland, New Zealand)
- International literacy and storytelling research

Building Your Own Resource Bank

Creating materials specific to your context

Documentation Approach

Start collecting evidence from your own practice:

- Video record story sessions (with permissions) for your own reflection
- Keep a simple journal of what works and what doesn't
- Photograph children's responses and engagement during stories
- Document examples of improved learning outcomes

Share with colleagues:

- Internal training sessions using your own examples
- Staff meeting demonstrations of successful story sessions

- Peer observation partnerships with other teachers
- Informal discussion groups about storytelling experiences

Collaborative Development

Work with your school team to:

- Create planning templates that fit your specific context
- Develop story collections relevant to your curriculum priorities
- Build assessment tools that work with your existing systems
- Design communication materials for your parent community

Connect with other schools:

- Local authority networks interested in creative pedagogy
- Initial teacher training partnerships where you might demonstrate practice
- Continuing professional development networks exploring narrative approaches
- Regional meetings of teachers interested in storytelling

Making Research Work for You

Start with What Interests You

Don't try to read everything. Focus on:

- Research that addresses your specific questions or challenges
- Studies involving age groups similar to your pupils
- Evidence relevant to your curriculum priorities
- Examples from contexts similar to your school

Apply Critically

Remember that research provides insights, not prescriptions:

- Consider how findings might apply to your specific children
- Adapt ideas rather than copying exactly
- Test approaches with your own classes before committing fully

- Trust your professional judgement alongside research evidence

Share Your Learning

When you find useful resources:

- Tell colleagues about helpful research or approaches
- Contribute to the Stories for Schools™ platform with your discoveries
- Write brief summaries for your school newsletter or staff briefings
- Present findings at local teacher networks or conferences

What You Can Access Now

Current Resources

- Basic planning templates and frameworks
- Contact information for Stories for Schools™ team
- Information about potential training and development opportunities
- Guidance on implementing the three-question framework

Future Developments

As the Stories for Schools™ programme grows, additional resources may become available:

- Expanded story collections with curriculum mapping
- Professional development materials
- Case studies from implementing schools
- Research updates and evidence summaries

Building Your Own Resource Network

Finding Storytelling Communities

Local Networks:

- Contact your local authority's English or Arts advisors
- Join regional storytelling societies or groups

- Attend education conferences that include narrative approaches
- Connect with local libraries and cultural organisations

Online Connections:

- Search social media for education hashtags like #storytelling #primaryteaching
- Join professional networks focused on creative pedagogy
- Follow education bloggers who write about narrative teaching
- Participate in online discussions about arts integration

Professional Development

Training Opportunities:

- Look for storytelling workshops offered by arts organisations
- Attend education conferences with sessions on narrative approaches
- Investigate university courses on children's literature or creative pedagogy
- Contact Stories for Schools™ about potential training visits

Self-Development:

- Read widely about storytelling in education
- Practice with willing colleagues or family members
- Attend storytelling events to observe techniques
- Document your own classroom experiences for reflection

Creating School-Based Support

Internal Networks:

- Start conversations with colleagues interested in creative teaching
- Organise informal sharing sessions about successful lessons
- Create planning partnerships with teachers in different year groups
- Document and share examples of effective story-based sessions

Leadership Engagement:

- Present evidence of storytelling's impact to senior leaders
- Invite headteachers to observe story sessions
- Include storytelling approaches in professional development discussions
- Connect narrative work to school improvement priorities

The Reality of Resource Development

Strategic storytelling in education is still developing as a field. This means:

Opportunities: You can contribute to developing the approach rather than just consuming existing materials

Challenges: Limited ready-made resources mean more work creating your own initially

Community: Teachers sharing experiences informally often provide the most practical support

Growth: The field will develop as more schools implement storytelling approaches successfully

Your early adoption of strategic storytelling makes you a pioneer. While this requires more initial effort, it also means you can shape how the approach develops and help other schools benefit from your experience.

Appendix

Story Sources and Variations

Where to find traditional tales and how to choose appropriate versions.

Traditional tales exist in multiple versions, shaped by different cultures, time periods, and storytelling traditions. This appendix helps you find reliable sources and choose versions appropriate for your classroom context and curriculum objectives.

Understanding Story Variations

Why Stories Have Multiple Versions

Traditional tales evolved through oral transmission across cultures and generations. Each telling adapted stories to local values, customs, and needs. Understanding this helps you:

- Choose versions that match your teaching objectives
- Respect cultural origins and variations
- Adapt stories appropriately for your context
- Understand why the same tale might feel different in different tellings

Types of Variations
Cultural Adaptations:

- Different character names and settings
- Varying moral emphases or conclusions
- Cultural-specific details and customs
- Regional language patterns and expressions

Historical Changes:

- Simplified language for modern audiences
- Adjusted content for contemporary sensitivities
- Changed social contexts (family structures, occupations)
- Updated cultural references and values

Educational Adaptations:

- Age-appropriate language and content
- Shortened or extended versions for different time allocations
- Curriculum-linked elements and vocabulary
- Visual or multimedia enhancements

Recommended Print Sources
Classic Collections
Grimm's Fairy Tales (Various Editions)

- **Best for:** European traditional tales, moral themes
- **Age range:** KS1-KS2 (choose edition carefully)
- **Curriculum links:** Character study, cultural heritage, historical context
- **Notes:** Many modern editions available with age-appropriate language

Aesop's Fables (Various Editions)

- **Best for:** Quick moral tales, discussion starters

- **Age range:** EYFS-KS2
- **Curriculum links:** PSHE, philosophy, character education
- **Notes:** Short format perfect for busy timetables

Joseph Jacobs - English Fairy Tales

- **Best for:** British traditional tales, cultural identity
- **Age range:** KS1-KS2
- **Curriculum links:** Local heritage, geography, history
- **Notes:** Includes familiar tales like *"Jack and the Beanstalk," "Goldilocks"*

Andrew Lang - The Colour Fairy Books

- **Best for:** International tale collections, cultural diversity
- **Age range:** KS2
- **Curriculum links:** Global awareness, cultural comparison
- **Notes:** Twelve volumes covering worldwide traditional tales

Contemporary Retellings

Kevin Crossley-Holland - British Folk Tales

- **Best for:** High-quality prose versions, literary merit
- **Age range:** Upper KS2
- **Curriculum links:** English literature, creative writing models
- **Notes:** Beautifully written, maintains traditional elements

Geraldine McCaughrean - Various Collections

- **Best for:** Accessible modern language, engaging storytelling
- **Age range:** KS1-KS2
- **Curriculum links:** Contemporary literature, storytelling techniques
- **Notes:** Award-winning author with gift for traditional tale retelling

Angela Carter - The Fairy Tales of Charles Perrault

- **Best for:** Literary analysis, sophisticated language

- **Age range:** Upper KS2 (teacher reference)
- **Curriculum links:** Historical literature, cultural studies
- **Notes:** More suitable for teacher background than direct classroom use

Multicultural Collections

Jamila Gavin - Tales from India

- **Best for:** South Asian traditional tales, cultural diversity
- **Age range:** KS1-KS2
- **Curriculum links:** Global citizenship, religious education
- **Notes:** Authentic retellings with cultural context

Grace Hallworth - Caribbean Folk Tales

- **Best for:** Caribbean storytelling traditions, oral heritage
- **Age range:** KS1-KS2
- **Curriculum links:** Cultural diversity, community traditions
- **Notes:** Strong rhythm and language patterns

Adèle Geras - My Grandmother's Stories (Jewish Tales)

- **Best for:** Jewish storytelling traditions, wisdom tales
- **Age range:** KS1-KS2
- **Curriculum links:** Religious education, cultural heritage
- **Notes:** Warm, family-centered stories with moral themes

Various - African Folk Tales Collections

- **Best for:** African storytelling traditions, diverse perspectives
- **Age range:** EYFS-KS2
- **Curriculum links:** Global awareness, cultural studies
- **Notes:** Many excellent collections available; check for authentic sources

Digital and Audio Sources

Project Gutenberg (www.gutenberg.org)

- **Content:** Public domain fairy tale and folklore collections
- **Advantages:** Free access, searchable, multiple formats
- **Considerations:** May need language updating for classroom use
- **Best for:** Teacher research and adaptation source material

Internet Archive (archive.org)

- **Content:** Historical children's books and audio recordings
- **Advantages:** Original illustrations, historical context
- **Considerations:** Copyright varies; check before classroom use
- **Best for:** Understanding story evolution and cultural context

BBC Sounds and BBC iPlayer

- **Content:** Professional storytelling recordings, educational programmes
- **Advantages:** High production quality, curriculum links
- **Considerations:** Availability may be time-limited
- **Best for:** Hearing professional storytelling techniques

Educational Platforms

Stories for Schools™ platform (www.storiesforschools.com)

- **Content:** Three-question frameworks applied to traditional tales
- **Advantages:** Designed specifically for strategic storytelling
- **Considerations:** Developing resource base
- **Best for:** Framework-aligned story planning

Choosing Appropriate Versions

Age Appropriateness

Early Years Foundation Stage:

- Simple language and clear moral themes

- Short duration (3-5 minutes telling time)
- Visual and participatory elements
- Familiar characters and situations

Key Stage 1:

- Slightly more complex plots and characters
- Opportunities for discussion and reflection
- Clear moral lessons with practical application
- Cultural diversity and different perspectives

Key Stage 2:

- Sophisticated themes and moral complexity
- Historical and cultural context
- Philosophical discussion opportunities
- Cross-curricular learning potential

Curriculum Alignment

Science Connections:

- Look for stories involving materials, forces, life cycles, or natural phenomena
- **Examples:** *"Three Little Pigs"* (materials), *"Jack and the Beanstalk"* (plant growth)

History Links:

- Choose tales that illuminate historical periods or social structures
- **Examples:** *"Stone Soup"* (community cooperation), *"Little Red Hen"* (agricultural society)

PSHE Themes:

- Select stories addressing relevant emotional and social learning objectives
- **Examples:** *"Ugly Duckling"* (identity), *"Boy Who Cried Wolf"* (honesty)

Geography Connections:
- Use tales from different cultures to explore global diversity
- **Examples:** Stories from various continents showing different environments

Cultural Sensitivity
Authentic Sources:
- Seek stories from authentic cultural sources
- Avoid appropriated or stereotypical versions
- Research cultural context and meaning
- Consult community members when possible

Respectful Adaptation:
- Maintain essential cultural elements
- Acknowledge story origins and traditions
- Avoid oversimplification or misrepresentation
- Consider inviting cultural community members to share stories

Inclusive Selection:
- Include stories from diverse cultural traditions
- Ensure representation reflects your school community
- Balance familiar and unfamiliar cultural contexts
- Address bias in traditional tale collections

Copyright and Usage Considerations
Public Domain Stories
Most traditional tales are in the public domain, meaning you can:
- Tell them freely in educational settings
- Adapt language and content for your classroom
- Create your own versions and extensions
- Use them for assessment and documentation

Modern Retellings

Contemporary versions may be under copyright protection:

- Check copyright status before extensive use
- Educational use often permitted under fair dealing
- Credit authors and illustrators appropriately
- Consider purchasing if using extensively

Digital Resources

- Verify licensing terms for digital materials
- Educational platforms often include usage rights
- Audio recordings may have separate copyright considerations
- Always credit sources appropriately

Creating Your Story Bank

Building Systematically

Start with Essentials: Begin with 5-10 stories that support your key curriculum areas and address universal themes like courage, kindness, perseverance, and fairness.

Add Gradually: Include one new story per month, focusing on:

- Cultural diversity and representation
- Specific curriculum support needs
- Children's interests and requests
- Seasonal or topical relevance

Organise Effectively:

- Digital folder system by theme or curriculum area
- Physical filing with quick-reference frameworks
- Cross-reference for multiple curriculum connections
- Notes on successful variations and adaptations

Quality Over Quantity

Know Your Core Stories Well:

- Practice telling until they feel natural
- Understand multiple curriculum applications
- Develop confidence with various extensions
- Document what works with different year groups

Adapt and Personalise:

- Modify language for your local context
- Include references children will understand
- Adjust length based on attention spans
- Add cultural elements relevant to your community

Share and Collaborate

With Colleagues:

- Exchange successful story-curriculum combinations
- Share adaptation techniques and improvements
- Plan coordinated approaches across year groups
- Support each other's storytelling development

With Community:

- Invite cultural storytellers to share traditions
- Learn from parents and community members
- Respect and incorporate local storytelling heritage
- Build bridges between school and community narratives

Troubleshooting Common Issues

"I Can't Find the Right Version"

Solution: Adapt existing versions rather than searching endlessly. Use the emotional core to guide modifications while maintaining story integrity.

"The Language Feels Too Old-Fashioned"

Solution: Update vocabulary while preserving story rhythm and essential elements. Focus on clarity without losing narrative magic.

"Cultural Context Seems Inappropriate"

Solution: Research authentic sources, consult community members, or choose different cultural versions that better match your context.

"Story Doesn't Match Curriculum Needs"

Solution: Remember that emotional cores are universal - look for natural connections rather than forcing artificial links.

Building Confidence

Start with stories you genuinely enjoy and understand. Your enthusiasm will compensate for any technical limitations while you develop skills and expand your repertoire.

The most important resource isn't the perfect version of every story - it's your commitment to using narrative purposefully to enhance children's learning and understanding of the world around them.

Good stories, well told with clear educational purpose, transform classrooms. These sources provide everything you need to begin that transformation with confidence and cultural respect.

REFERENCES

Alexander, R. (2008). *Essays on Pedagogy.* Routledge.

Alexander, R. (2020). *A Dialogic Teaching Companion.* Routledge.

Bishop, R.S. (1990). Mirrors, windows, and sliding glass doors. *Perspectives,* 1(3), ix-xi.

Bruner, J. (1986). *Actual Minds, Possible Worlds.* Harvard University Press.

Bruner, J. (1991). Acts of meaning. *Harvard University Press.*

Burger, K. & Winner, E. (2013). Instruction in visual art: Can it help children learn to read? *Journal of Aesthetic Education,* 47(3), 24-46.

Carter, A. (1977). *The Fairy Tales of Charles Perrault.* Victor Gollancz.

Cremin, T. (2009). *Teaching English Creatively.* Routledge.

Crossley-Holland, K. (1987). *British Folk Tales: New Versions.* Orchard Books.

Centre for Literacy in Primary Education. (2023). *The Power of Reading in the Early Years: Evidence of impact.* CLPE

Department for Education (2019). *Education inspection framework.* DfE.

Durlak, J.A., Weissberg, R.P., Dymnicki, A.B., Taylor, R.D. & Schellinger, K.B. (2011). The impact of enhancing students' social and emotional learning: A meta-analysis of school-based universal interventions. *Child Development,* 82(1), 405-432.

Education Endowment Foundation (2021). *Arts participation.* EEF.

Egan, K. (1986). *Teaching as Story Telling: An Alternative Approach to Teaching and Curriculum in the Elementary School.* University of Chicago Press.

Fletcher, A. (2021). *Story Thinking: The New Science of Narrative Intelligence.* Columbia University Press.

Gavin, J. (2017). *Tales from India.* Templar Books.

Gay, G. (2018). *Culturally Responsive Teaching: Theory, Research, and Practice* (3rd ed.). Teachers College Press.

Geras, A. (1990). *My Grandmother's Stories: A Collection of Jewish Folk Tales.* Knopf Books for Young Readers.

Gottschall, J. (2012). *The Storytelling Animal: How Stories Make Us Human.* Houghton Mifflin Harcourt.

Grimm, J. & Grimm, W. (Various editions). *Grimm's Fairy Tales.* Multiple publishers.

Hallworth, G. (1996). *Listen to This Story: Tales from the Caribbean.* Methuen.

Hasson, U., Ghazanfar, A.A., Galantucci, B., Garrod, S. & Keysers, C. (2012). Brain-to-brain coupling: A mechanism for creating and sharing a social world. *Trends in Cognitive Sciences,* 16(2), 114-121.

Haven, K. (2007). *Story Proof: The Science Behind the Startling Power of Story.* Libraries Unlimited.

Heath, S.B. (1983). *Ways with Words: Language, Life and Work in Communities and Classrooms.* Cambridge University Press.

Immordino-Yang, M.H. (2016). *Emotions, Learning, and the Brain: Exploring the Educational Implications of Affective Neuroscience.* W.W. Norton.

Jacobs, J. (1890). *English Fairy Tales.* David Nutt.

Lang, A. (1889-1910). *The Colour Fairy Books* (12 volumes). Longmans, Green & Co.

McCaughrean, G. (Various collections). Multiple publishers.

Oates, J. & Grayson, A. (2020). *Cognitive and language development in children.* Cambridge University Press.

OECD (2018). *PISA 2018 Reading Framework.* OECD Publishing.

Ofsted (2025). *Education Inspection Framework.* Crown Copyright.

Robledo, J. & Ham, V. (2013). Making reading accessible for students with autism: Creating comprehensive school reading programmes. *Teaching Exceptional Children,* 45(3), 40-48.

Willingham, D.T. (2009). Why Don't Students Like School? A Cognitive Scientist Answers Questions About How the Mind Works and What It Means for the Classroom. Jossey-Bass.

Zak, P.J. (2014). Why inspiring stories make us react: The neuroscience of narrative. *Cerebrum,* 2014, 2.

About Us

Sita Brand

Artistic Director/CEO Sita studied Drama at University. She came to Settle following an extensive career in the arts and founded Settle Stories in 2010. Sita is passionate about traditional myths and folktales and exploring how we can use new technology to share them with wider audiences. Sita is a teacher of mindfulness and meditation and brings this to Settle Stories through retreats. Sita also works as a performance storyteller, a Buddhist Chaplain and is a Trustee at the York Museums Trust.

Emma Thompson

Emma is a trained primary school teacher and brings her many years of experience in education, including middle leadership roles, to her role in managing the development of our children's mental health programme that brings together storytelling, mindfulness exercises, and creative activities. This programme is designed to foster the wellbeing of our children and equip them with the tools to build resilience. In addition to her work on the programme, Emma also manages Settle Stories' wonderful network of volunteers.

Settle Stories

Founded in 2010, Settle Stories is a registered charity based in the Yorkshire Dales. We use the irreplaceable human art of storytelling to promote empathy and critical thinking in our divided, AI-driven world. Through live performances, digital tools, and creative education, we help people everywhere listen more deeply, think more creatively, and find common ground across cultures. Storytelling that educates, empowers, and endures. This is Settle Stories.

info@settlestories.org.uk

www.ingramcontent.com/pod-product-compliance
Lightning Source LLC
Chambersburg PA
CBHW041823220426
43666CB00004BA/58